Structure and Properties of Matter

elevate science

MODULES

SAVVAS

LEARNING COMPANY

You're an author!

As you write in this science book, your answers and personal discoveries will be recorded for you to keep, making this book unique to you. That is why you are one of the primary authors of this book.

✏️ **In the space below, print your name, school, town, and state. Then write a short autobiography that includes your interests and accomplishments.**

YOUR NAME ....

SCHOOL ....

TOWN, STATE ....

AUTOBIOGRAPHY ....

....

Your Photo

The cover photo shows the Strokkur Geyser about to errupt.

Front cover: Geyser, Frank Krahmer/Getty Images; Back cover: Science Doodle, LHF Graphics/Shutterstock.

LEARNING COMPANY

ISBN-13: 978-1-418-29151-8
ISBN-10:   1-418-29151-X
8   22

Program Authors

ZIPPORAH MILLER, Ed.D.
Coordinator for K-12 Science Programs, Anne Arundel County Public Schools
Dr. Zipporah Miller currently serves as the Senior Manager for Organizational Learning with the Anne Arundel County Public School System. Prior to that she served as the K-12 Coordinator for science in Anne Arundel County. She conducts national training to science stakeholders on the Next Generation Science Standards. Dr. Miller also served as the Associate Executive Director for Professional Development Programs and conferences at the National Science Teachers Association (NSTA) and served as a reviewer during the development of Next Generation Science Standards. Dr. Miller holds a doctoral degree from the University of Maryland College Park, a master's degree in school administration and supervision from Bowie State University and a bachelor's degree from Chadron State College.

MICHAEL J. PADILLA, Ph.D.
Professor Emeritus, Eugene P. Moore School of Education, Clemson University, Clemson, South Carolina
Michael J. Padilla taught science in middle and secondary schools, has more than 30 years of experience educating middle-school science teachers, and served as one of the writers of the 1996 U.S. National Science Education Standards. In recent years Mike has focused on teaching science to English Language Learners. His extensive experience as Principal Investigator on numerous National Science Foundation and U.S. Department of Education grants resulted in more than $35 million in funding to improve science education. He served as president of the National Science Teachers Association, the world's largest science teaching organization, in 2005–6.

MICHAEL E. WYSESSION, Ph.D
Professor of Earth and Planetary Sciences, Washington University, St. Louis, Missouri
Author of more than 100 science and science education publications, Dr. Wysession was awarded the prestigious National Science Foundation Presidential Faculty Fellowship and Packard Foundation Fellowship for his research in geophysics, primarily focused on using seismic tomography to determine the forces driving plate tectonics. Dr. Wysession is also a leader in geoscience literacy and education; he is the chair of the Earth Science Literacy Initiative, the author of several popular video lectures on geology in the *Great Courses* series, and a lead writer of the *Next Generation Science Standards**.

---

*Next Generation Science Standards is a registered trademark of WestEd. Neither WestEd nor the lead states and partners that developed the Next Generation Science Standards were involved in the production of this product, and do not endorse it. NGSS Lead States. 2013. *Next Generation Science Standards: For States, By States.* Washington, DC: The National Academies Press.

REVIEWERS

Program Consultants

Carol Baker
Science Curriculum

Dr. Carol K. Baker is superintendent for Lyons Elementary K-8 School District in Lyons, Illinois. Prior to this, she was Director of Curriculum for Science and Music in Oak Lawn, Illinois. Before this she taught Physics and Earth Science for 18 years. In the recent past, Dr. Baker also wrote assessment questions for ACT (EXPLORE and PLAN), was elected president of the Illinois Science Teachers Association from 2011–2013, and served as a member of the Museum of Science and Industry (Chicago) advisory board. She is a writer of the Next Generation Science Standards. Dr. Baker received her B.S. in Physics and a science teaching certification. She completed her master's of Educational Administration (K-12) and earned her doctorate in Educational Leadership.

Jim Cummins
ELL

Dr. Cummins's research focuses on literacy development in multilingual schools and the role technology plays in learning across the curriculum. *Elevate Science* incorporates research-based principles for integrating language with the teaching of academic content based on Dr. Cummins's work.

Elfrieda Hiebert
Literacy

Dr. Hiebert, a former primary-school teacher, is President and CEO of TextProject, a non-profit aimed at providing open-access resources for instruction of beginning and struggling readers, She is also a research associate at the University of California Santa Cruz. Her research addresses how fluency, vocabulary, and knowledge can be fostered through appropriate texts, and her contributions have been recognized through awards such as the Oscar Causey Award for Outstanding Contributions to Reading Research (Literacy Research Association, 2015), Research to Practice award (American Educational Research Association, 2013), and the William S. Gray Citation of Merit Award for Outstanding Contributions to Reading Research (International Reading Association, 2008).

Content Reviewers

Alex Blom, Ph.D.
Associate Professor
Department Of Physical Sciences
Alverno College
Milwaukee, Wisconsin

Joy Branlund, Ph.D.
Department of Physical Science
Southwestern Illinois College
Granite City, Illinois

Judy Calhoun
Associate Professor
Physical Sciences
Alverno College
Milwaukee, Wisconsin

Stefan Debbert
Associate Professor of Chemistry
Lawrence University
Appleton, Wisconsin

Diane Doser
Professor
Department of Geological Sciences
University of Texas at El Paso
El Paso, Texas

Rick Duhrkopf, Ph.D.
Department of Biology
Baylor University
Waco, Texas

Jennifer Liang
University of Minnesota Duluth
Duluth, Minnesota

Heather Mernitz, Ph.D.
Associate Professor of Physical Sciences
Alverno College
Milwaukee, Wisconsin

Joseph McCullough, Ph.D.
Cabrillo College
Aptos, California

Katie M. Nemeth, Ph.D.
Assistant Professor
College of Science and Engineering
University of Minnesota Duluth
Duluth, Minnesota

Maik Pertermann
Department of Geology
Western Wyoming Community College
Rock Springs, Wyoming

Scott Rochette
Department of the Earth Sciences
The College at Brockport
 State University of New York
Brockport, New York

David Schuster
Washington University in St Louis
St. Louis, Missouri

Shannon Stevenson
Department of Biology
University of Minnesota Duluth
Duluth, Minnesota

Paul Stoddard, Ph.D.
Department of Geology and
 Environmental Geosciences
Northern Illinois University
DeKalb, Illinois

Nancy Taylor
American Public University
Charles Town, West Virginia

Teacher Reviewers

Jennifer Bennett, M.A.
Memorial Middle School
Tampa, Florida

Sonia Blackstone
Lake County Schools
Howey In the Hills, Florida

Teresa Bode
Roosevelt Elementary
Tampa, Florida

Tyler C. Britt, Ed.S.
Curriculum & Instructional
 Practice Coordinator
Raytown Quality Schools
Raytown, Missouri

A. Colleen Campos
Grandview High School
Aurora, Colorado

Ronald Davis
Riverview Elementary
Riverview, Florida

Coleen Doulk
Challenger School
Spring Hill, Florida

Mary D. Dube
Burnett Middle School
Seffner, Florida

Sandra Galpin
Adams Middle School
Tampa, Florida

Margaret Henry
Lebanon Junior High School
Lebanon, Ohio

Christina Hill
Beth Shields Middle School
Ruskin, Florida

Judy Johnis
Gorden Burnett Middle School
Seffner, Florida

Karen Y. Johnson
Beth Shields Middle School
Ruskin, Florida

Jane Kemp
Lockhart Elementary School
Tampa, Florida

Denise Kuhling
Adams Middle School
Tampa, Florida

Esther Leonard, M.Ed. and L.M.T.
Gifted and talented Implementation Specialist
San Antonio Independent School District
San Antonio, Texas

Kelly Maharaj
Challenger K–8 School of Science
 and Mathematics
Spring Hill, Florida

Kevin J. Maser, Ed.D.
H. Frank Carey Jr/Sr High School
Franklin Square, New York

Angie L. Matamoros, Ph.D.
ALM Science Consultant
Weston, Florida

Corey Mayle
Brogden Middle School
Durham, North Carolina

Keith McCarthy
George Washington Middle School
Wayne, New Jersey

Yolanda O. Peña
John F. Kennedy Junior High School
West Valley City, Utah

Kathleen M. Poe
Jacksonville Beach Elementary School
Jacksonville Beach, Florida

Wendy Rauld
Monroe Middle School
Tampa, Florida

Anne Rice
Woodland Middle School
Gurnee, Illinois

Bryna Selig
Gaithersburg Middle School
Gaithersburg, Maryland

Pat (Patricia) Shane, Ph.D.
STEM & ELA Education Consultant
Chapel Hill, North Carolina

Diana Shelton
Burnett Middle School
Seffner, Florida

Nakia Sturrup
Jennings Middle School
Seffner, Florida

Melissa Triebwasser
Walden Lake Elementary
Plant City, Florida

Michele Bubley Wiehagen
Science Coach
Miles Elementary School
Tampa, Florida

Pauline Wilcox
Instructional Science Coach
Fox Chapel Middle School
Spring Hill, Florida

Safety Reviewers

Douglas Mandt, M.S.
Science Education Consultant
Edgewood, Washington

Juliana Textley, Ph.D.
Author, NSTA books on school science safety
Adjunct Professor
Lesley University
Cambridge, Massachusetts

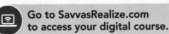

Go to SavvasRealize.com
to access your digital course.

▶ **VIDEO**
• Museum Technician

👆 **INTERACTIVITY**
• What Makes Up Matter?
• Molecules and Extended Structures
• Calculating Density
• Weight on the Moon
• Properties of Matter

📱 **VIRTUAL LAB**
• What's the Matter with My Chocolate?

☑ **ASSESSMENT**

📖 **eTEXT**

HANDS-ON LABS

Connect The Nuts and Bolts of Formulas

Investigate
• Models of Atoms and Molecules
• Observing Physical Properties
• Physical and Chemical Changes

Demonstrate
Help Out the Wildlife

Go to SavvasRealize.com to access your digital course.

VIDEO
• Materials Scientist

INTERACTIVITY
• Particles and States of Matter
• Properties of Solids, Liquids, and Gases
• A Matter of Printing
• Particle Motion and States of Matter
• States of Matter
• Thermal Energy and Changes of State
• Gas Laws
• Hot Air Balloon Ride

VIRTUAL LAB
• Cooking and the States of Matter

ASSESSMENT

eTEXT

HANDS-ON LABS

иConnect Solid, Liquid, or Gas?
иInvestigate
• Properties of Matter
• Mirror, Mirror
• Testing Charles's and Boyle's Laws

иDemonstrate
Melting Ice

Elevate your thinking!

Elevate Science takes science to a whole new level and lets you take ownership of your learning. Explore science in the world around you. Investigate how things work. Think critically and solve problems! *Elevate Science* helps you think like a scientist, so you're ready for a world of discoveries.

Explore Your World

Explore real-life scenarios with engaging Quests that dig into science topics around the world. You can:

- Solve real-world problems
- Apply skills and knowledge
- Communicate solutions

Quest KICKOFF

What do you think is causing Pleasant Pond to turn green?

In 2016, algal blooms turned bodies of water green and slimy in Florida, Utah, California, and 17 other states. These blooms put people and ecosystems in danger. Scientists, such as limnologists, are working to predict and prevent future algal blooms. In this problem-based Quest activity, you will investigate an algal bloom at a lake and determine its cause. In labs and digital activities, you will apply what you learn in each lesson to help you gather evidence to solve the mystery. With enough evidence, you will be able to identify what you believe is the cause of the algal bloom and present a solution in the Findings activity.

Make Connections

Elevate Science connects science to other subjects and shows you how to better understand the world through:

- Mathematics
- Reading and Writing
- Literacy

Math Toolbox

Graphing Population Changes

Ohio's Deer Population

Changes in a population over time, such as white-tailed deer in Ohio, can be displayed in a graph.

Deer Population Trends, 2000–2010

Year	Population (estimated)	Year	Population (estimated)
2000	525,000	2006	770,000
2001	560,000	2007	725,000
2002	620,000	2008	745,000
2003	670,000	2009	750,000
2004	715,000	2010	710,000
2005	720,000		

Relationships Use the data

800,000

READING CHECK Determine Central ideas

What adaptations might the giraffe have that help it survive in its environment?

Academic Vocabulary

Relate the term *decomposer* to the verb *compose*. What does it mean to compose something?

Build Skills for the Future

- Master the Engineering Design Process
- Apply critical thinking and analytical skills
- Learn about STEM careers

Focus on Inquiry

Case studies put you in the shoes of a scientist to solve real-world mysteries using real data. You will be able to:

- Analyze Data
- Test a hypothesis
- Solve the Case

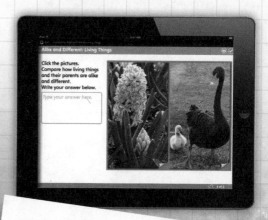

Case Study

MS-LS2-1

THE CASE OF THE DISAPPEARING

Cerulean Warbler

The cerulean warbler is a small, migratory songbird named for its blue color. Cerulean warblers breed in eastern North America during the spring and summer. The warblers spend the winter months in the Andes Mountains of Colombia, Venezuela, Ecuador, and Peru in northern part of South America.

Enter the Lab

Hands-on experiments and virtual labs help you test ideas and show what you know in performance-based assessments. Scaffolded labs include:

- STEM Labs
- Design Your Own
- Open-ended Labs

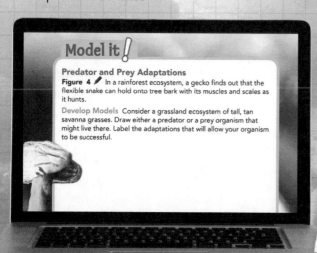

Model it

Predator and Prey Adaptations

Figure 4 In a rainforest ecosystem, a gecko finds out that the flexible snake can hold onto tree bark with its muscles and scales as it hunts.

Develop Models Consider a grassland ecosystem of tall, tan savanna grasses. Draw either a predator or a prey organism that might live there. Label the adaptations that will allow your organism to be successful.

HANDS-ON LAB

μInvestigate Observe how once-living matter is broken down into smaller components in the process of decomposition.

Introduction to Matter

NGSS PERFORMANCE EXPECTATIONS

MS-PS1-1 Develop models to describe the atomic composition of simple molecules and extended structures.

MS-PS1-2 Analyze and interpret data on the properties of substances before and after the substances interact to determine if a chemical reaction has occurred.

How did this ice form?

GO ONLINE
to access your
digital course

 VIDEO

 INTERACTIVITY

 VIRTUAL LAB

 ASSESSMENT

 eTEXT

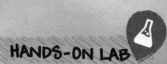 HANDS-ON LAB

HANDS-ON LAB

иConnect See how you can model particles that are so small you can't see them.

The Essential Question

How can we observe, measure, and use matter?

CCC Energy and Matter If you step outside when the temperature is well below freezing, you can bet it will not be raining. You are more likely to see snow if there is any precipitation at all. Water in the clouds is so cold that it turns into ice crystals. What are some of the physical differences between rain water and ice crystals such as snow?

....

....

....

....

....

Quest KICKOFF

How can you use science to make special effects?

Phenomenon A special effects company would like to be chosen to develop the special effects for a new movie. But first, the movie director wants to check out the company's capabilities. In this problem-based Quest activity, you will develop a movie scene that uses some amazing special effects. You will write the script and the storyboards. As you develop the special effects, you will explore different types of substances that are used to make special effects. You will understand the role that physical and chemical properties of matter play in the special effects. Finally, you will present your scene, along with an explanation of the special effects and the properties of matter behind them.

NBC LEARN ▶ VIDEO

After watching the Quest Kickoff video about special effects, complete the sentences about special effects you have seen in movies. Then discuss your answers with a partner.

1 One special effect I have seen is

....

....

....

2 It added to the scene because

....

....

....

👆 **INTERACTIVITY**

Lights! Camera! Action!

MS-PS1-2 Analyze and interpret data on the properties of substances before and after the substances interact to determine if a chemical reaction has occurred.

Quest CHECK-IN

IN LESSON 1

How can substance changes play a role in special effects? Think about how you can take advantage of physical and chemical changes to create special effects.

👆 **INTERACTIVITY**

The Science of Special Effects

IN LESSON 2

How will the amounts of substances affect physical and chemical changes? Consider the amounts of substances you will need to create the special effects you want.

Quest CHECK-INS

IN LESSON 3

How do substances interact? Explore substances and how they interact. Collect and analyze data to help develop your special effects.

👆 **INTERACTIVITY**

Mysterious Movie Fog

HANDS-ON LAB

Cinematic Science

Smoke in movie scenes can be eye-catching and dramatic, but it is never accidental. Directors carefully manage the production and movement of the smoke to create the desired effect.

Quest FINDINGS

Complete the Quest!

Present your scene and storyboard, and include an explanation of the physical and chemical changes involved in your special effects.

👆 **INTERACTIVITY**

Reflect on Your Scene

The Nuts and Bolts of Formulas

Background

Phenomenon Have you ever noticed dust particles floating through the air? You may think nothing is smaller than a dust particle, but in fact, everything you see is made up of atoms that form molecules of substances. The atoms and molecules are many times smaller than dust particles. How can you describe something you cannot see? In this lab, you will develop a model that describes a molecule.

> How can you **develop a model** of particles that are so small you can't even see them?

Materials

(per group)

- short bolt
- long bolt
- hex nuts
- square nuts

Develop and Use a Model

☐ **1. SEP Develop a Model** Examine the objects supplied by your teacher. Assign a symbol to each type of object. Record your assigned symbols.

☐ **2.** Assemble different structures using the objects you have. In the space provided, sketch your structures.

☐ **3. SEP Use a Model** Under each sketch, write a formula for each structure using the symbols you assigned in Step 1.

☐ **4.** Share the symbols you assigned to each object with another group. Write a formula using those symbols and ask the other group to build the structure.

Sketch

HANDS-ON LAB

Connect Go online for a downloadable worksheet of this lab.

Analyze and Interpret Data

1. **SEP Design Solutions** Explain how you can assemble more than four structures even though you only have four kinds of objects.

   ....

   ....

   ....

   ....

2. **SEP Use Models** How can you assemble two different structures using 1 long bolt, 1 hex nut, and 1 square nut?

   ....

   ....

   ....

   ....

3. **SEP Develop and Use a Model** An acid has a formula of the form HA, where H is hydrogen and A is another kind of atom. A base has a formula of the form BOH, where H is hydrogen, O is oxygen, and B is another kind of atom. When AH and BOH combine water and something else form. Use a model to show this reaction and to predict the other substance.

Describing and Classifying Matter

Guiding Questions

- What is matter made of?
- What properties describe matter?
- How can you classify different types of matter?

Connection

Literacy Integrate With Visuals

MS-PS1-1

HANDS-ON LAB

и**Investigate** Develop your own models of atoms and molecules.

Vocabulary

matter
substance
physical property
chemical property
atom
element
molecule
compound
mixture

Academic Vocabulary

distill

Connect It !

✏️ **Several substances are shown in Figure 1. Two of the substances are in two different forms. Label these substances and each of their forms on the image.**

SEP Analyze Data Is there any matter in **Figure 1** that you cannot see?

....

Form a Hypothesis What substance might impact the formation of volcanic rock?

....

Matter

Anything that has mass and takes up space is **matter**. Wood, metal, paper, glass, cloth, plastic, and air are all matter. In fact, you are made of matter, too. We classify different types of matter by their properties. Some matter is visible, some is not. Some types of matter are usually found in liquid form, and others are usually solid. Chemistry is the study of matter and how it changes.

One of the first steps in classifying matter is to determine whether something is a **substance**—a single kind of matter that always has a specific makeup, or composition. For example, sodium chloride is a substance that we know as table salt. It is considered a pure substance because its composition is the same whether you're looking at a single grain of salt or a boulder of salt taken from a salt mine. Sea salt, on the other hand, which is formed when seawater evaporates, is not a pure substance. There are many other substances in seawater, and those substances are left behind with sodium chloride when the water evaporates.

Matter on Earth
Figure 1 Hot lava cools in the ocean to form this volcanic island.

VIDEO

Learn more about physical and chemical properties.

Physical Properties Whether you have a pure substance, such as gold, or a mixture, such as seawater, how it behaves and interacts with other substances depends on its properties. A **physical property** is a characteristic that can be observed without changing the matter into another type of matter. For example, gold melts at 1,064°C and boils at 2,856°C. It is an excellent conductor, meaning electricity moves through it very easily. Gold also has a high luster, or shininess, and a distinctive color. All of these characteristics are physical properties. They can be observed without changing the gold into something else.

Physical and Chemical Properties

Figure 2 Can you tell physical and chemical properties apart?

1. **SEP Evaluate Information** Analyze the photos and read their captions. Write "physical" or "chemical" next to "Property".

2. **SEP Engage in Argument** Below each photo, cite evidence that guided you to classify the properties as physical or chemical.

Water and carbon dioxide in the leaves of the coconut palm tree are converted to oxygen and sugar, thanks to the energy provided by the sun.

Oxygen is a substance that dissolves in water. Fish absorb oxygen from the water. When dissolved oxygen levels are low, it can be hard for organisms to survive.

Property

Evidence

....

....

....

Property

Evidence

....

....

....

Chemical Properties Other properties can only be observed by combining or breaking apart substances. These are **chemical properties**—characteristics that describe something's ability to become something else. For example, if you inject carbon dioxide gas into liquid water, some of the water will react with the carbon dioxide to produce carbonic acid. This ability to react is a chemical property of water. Likewise, the ability of carbon dioxide to combine with water and become carbonic acid is a chemical property.

Look at the images in **Figure 2** and read their captions. The images and captions will help you determine whether chemical or physical properties are being described.

☑ READING CHECK **Infer** Flammability is a measure of how easily something burns. Is this a physical or chemical property? Explain, using an example.

....

....

....

....

Literacy Connection

Integrate With Visuals As you determine whether the images and descriptions involve physical or chemical properties, set up a two-column table in your notebook in which you can record and classify examples of physical and chemical properties.

▤ **Reflect** Think of two substances that aren't mentioned on these pages. Name a physical and chemical property for each one.

If iron is exposed to air and water, it can rust.

Property

Evidence

....

....

....

Wood tends to be hard and relatively inflexible, especially when it's been dried. This is why wood is an excellent building material.

Property

Evidence

....

....

....

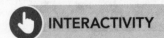
Components of Matter

There are a lot of tiny particles we can see, such as grains of sand. Have you ever wondered whether these tiny grains have even smaller particles inside? They do! The particle theory of matter explains that all matter is made up of very tiny particles called atoms.

Atoms An **atom** is the basic unit from which all matter is made. Different substances are made up of different types of atoms. But all atoms have the same basic structure. An atom has a positively charged center, or nucleus, containing smaller particles. Negatively charged particles circle around the nucleus and form a cloud of negative charge.

Elements Substances that are made up of only one type of atom are called **elements**. For instance, the element aluminum is made of only aluminum atoms, and no other pure substance has atoms like aluminum's atoms. Each element can be identified by its specific physical and chemical properties. You may already be familiar with some elements such as gold, oxygen, and carbon (**Figure 3**). These cannot be broken down into different substances. Elements are represented by one- or two-letter symbols, such as O for oxygen and Al for aluminum.

Atoms Combining

Figure 3 Diamond and graphite are extended structures of the same element: carbon. Diamond, the hardest natural substance, forms under intense pressure, with atoms packed tightly together. Carbon atoms form layers in graphite which easily slide and break off.

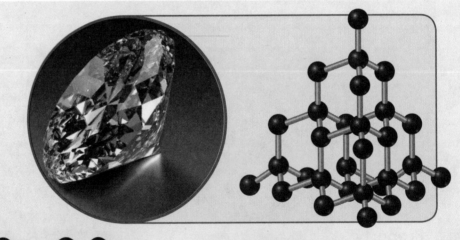

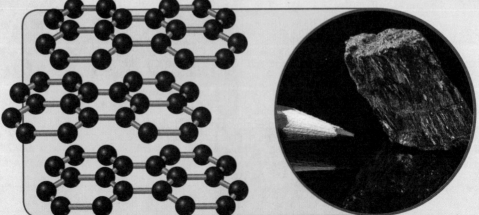

Molecules Most atoms can combine with other atoms. When this happens, a chemical bond forms. A chemical bond is a force of attraction between two or more atoms. Sometimes, atoms combine to form extended structures. One type of extended structure is a molecule. A **molecule** is a group of two or more atoms held together by chemical bonds. A molecule of carbon dioxide, as shown in **Figure 4** for example, is made up of a carbon atom chemically bonded to two oxygen atoms. Two atoms of the same element can also combine to form a molecule. For example, a hydrogen molecule is made up of two hydrogen atoms. Some large molecules are made of thousands of atoms!

HANDS-ON LAB

🔎Investigate Develop your own models of atoms and molecules.

Model It !

Molecules and Atoms

Figure 4 Explain Phenomena The four molecules shown here are made of different combinations of carbon, oxygen, or hydrogen atoms. Below each molecule, list the types of atoms in it and how many atoms there are of each type. The first answer is completed as an example.

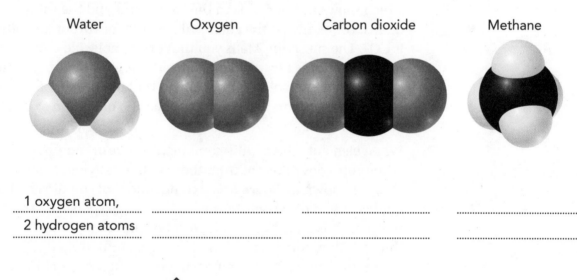

| Water | Oxygen | Carbon dioxide | Methane |

1 oxygen atom,
2 hydrogen atoms

SEP Develop Models 🖊
Draw a model of a two-atom molecule of hydrogen and label the atoms.

C₂H₆O

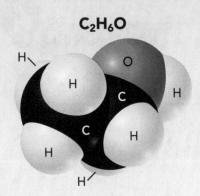

Compound From Corn
Figure 5 Ethanol is a chemical compound made from sugars in corn and other plants. It can be burned to power engines.

👆 **INTERACTIVITY**

Develop models of extended structures including molecules.

Compounds When a molecule contains more than one element, it is called a compound. A **compound** is a substance made of two or more elements that are chemically combined in a set ratio. A compound is represented by a chemical formula, which shows the elements in the compound and the ratio of atoms. For example, the chemical formula for carbon dioxide is CO_2. The subscript 2 tells you that every molecule of carbon dioxide contains two oxygen atoms. If there is no number after an element's symbol, it is understood that the number is 1. In CO_2, there is one carbon atom. The ratio of carbon to oxygen is 1 to 2.

When elements chemically combine, they form compounds with properties different from those of the individual elements. Ethanol, shown in **Figure 5**, is a compound that contains carbon, but because it also contains hydrogen and oxygen, and the molecule has a particular shape, it has different properties than the pure forms of carbon, hydrogen, and oxygen. There are many different compounds made of different combinations and configurations of those three elements.

☑ READING CHECK **Integrate With Visuals** How are pure carbon, oxygen, and hydrogen different from the compound ethanol which contains all three of those elements?

....

....

....

....

Types of Mixtures

You have learned that elements and compounds are substances. Most of the things found in nature, however, are not simple elements or compounds—they are mixtures. A **mixture** is made up of two or more substances that are together in the same place, but their atoms are not chemically bonded.

Mixtures differ from compounds. Each substance in a mixture keeps its own properties. Also, the parts of a mixture are not necessarily combined in a set ratio. Look at **Figure 6A**, which shows a bowl of mixed nuts. They are mixed together, but they are not chemically bonded to each other. This type of mixture is known as a heterogeneous mixture.

A homogeneous mixture is different from a heterogeneous mixture. In a homogeneous mixture, it is difficult or impossible to see the different parts. Combining dry ingredients for baking results in a homogeneous mixture, as shown in **Figure 6B**. Air is another homogeneous mixture, made of gases rather than solids. You know that oxygen is present in the air because you are able to breathe, but you cannot pinpoint exactly where the oxygen is in the air. A solution is a liquid example of a homogeneous mixture. Salt water is an example of a solution.

If you want to separate a mixture, you need to divide its parts according to their properties. This is possible because the substances in a mixture retain their own properties. The methods you can use to separate the parts of a mixture include distillation, evaporation, filtration, and magnetic attraction.

Magnetic attraction involves holding a magnet near a mixture to pull out anything that is attracted to the magnet, such as a metal. Evaporation is a good way to separate dissolved or suspended substances from water. This is how sea salt is harvested from the ocean. In filtration, a substance is passed through some kind of filter that allows fine particles, such as molecules of water, to pass through while filtering out larger particles. **Distillation** involves separating liquids by boiling them. The liquid with the lower boiling point will vaporize first, leaving the other liquid behind.

✓ **READING CHECK** **Apply Scientific Reasoning** Think about a lake. Would you describe it as a homogeneous mixture, a heterogeneous mixture, or both? Explain.

....

....

....

Heterogeneous and Homogeneous Mixtures

Figure 6 A bowl of mixed nuts is a heterogeneous mixture. You could easily separate the nuts by type. A bowl of cake mix is a homogeneous mixture. You could not easily separate the flour in the mix from the other dry ingredients.

Academic Vocabulary

Someone may ask you to distill a complicated idea into a brief summary that gets right to the point. How does this relate to distillation in chemistry?

....

....

....

Ammonia

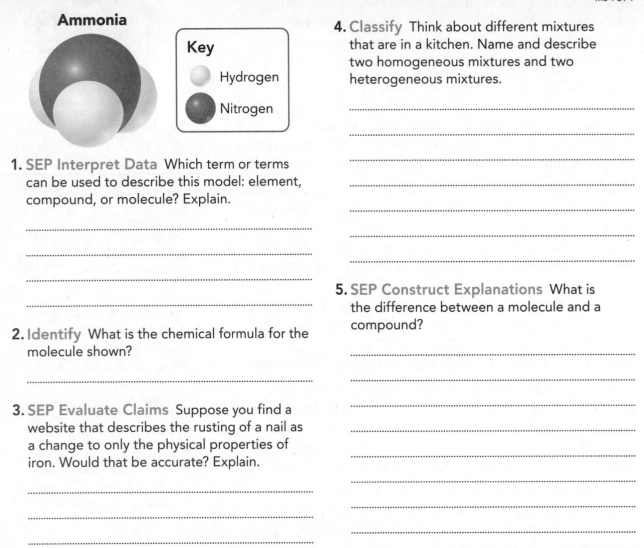

Key

○ Hydrogen

● Nitrogen

1. SEP Interpret Data Which term or terms can be used to describe this model: element, compound, or molecule? Explain.

....

....

....

....

2. Identify What is the chemical formula for the molecule shown?

....

3. SEP Evaluate Claims Suppose you find a website that describes the rusting of a nail as a change to only the physical properties of iron. Would that be accurate? Explain.

....

....

....

4. Classify Think about different mixtures that are in a kitchen. Name and describe two homogeneous mixtures and two heterogeneous mixtures.

....

....

....

....

....

....

....

5. SEP Construct Explanations What is the difference between a molecule and a compound?

....

....

....

....

....

....

....

....

Quest CHECK-IN

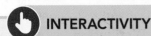

In this lesson, you learned about the properties that are used to describe matter. You also learned about mixtures and how they are classified as well as how their components can be separated.

SEP Define Problems Why is it important to know what substances you have available to work with, and how they might change, when developing special effects?

....

....

....

....

✋ INTERACTIVITY

The Science of Special Effects

Go online to learn about how different substances can be combined in various ways to achieve different outcomes.

Saving the World's Art

The world is full of works of art, from the delicate to the majestic, from the ancient to the new. Many are made of organic materials, such as paint, wood, and some stone. These materials are sensitive to changes in temperature and humidity. They break down as they age, just as living creatures do. This is where the museum technicians come in! It's their job to restore works of art.

If you are strongly interested in both science and art, a career as a museum technician might be perfect for you! It combines an appreciation of art, architecture, and sculpture with a detailed knowledge of the chemistry that breaks down artwork so that it can be restored to its original beauty.

VIDEO

Learn how a museum technician restores pieces of art.

MY CAREER

Type "museum technician" into an online search engine to learn more about this career.

Before

After

This is a painting on the ceiling on the Sistine Chapel after restoration. The inset shows what it looked like before.

2 Measuring Matter

Guiding Questions

- How can matter be measured?
- What properties of matter can be determined through measurement?

Connections

Literacy Cite Textual Evidence

Math Draw Comparative Inferences

MS-PS1-2

HANDS-ON LAB

uInvestigate Explore the physical properties of mass, volume, and density.

Vocabulary

mass
volume
weight
density

Academic Vocabulary

convert

Connect It!

✎ In the fruit market photo, outline three things that have mass.

Hypothesize How much do you think an apple weighs?

....

CCC Scale, Proportion, and Quantity How do you think an object's mass relates to its weight?

....

....

....

Expressing Weight, Mass, and Volume

Recall that matter is anything that has mass and takes up space. **Mass** is the amount of matter in an object. An object's mass does not change even if the force of gravity upon the object changes. The amount of space that matter occupies is called its **volume**. All forms of matter—solids, liquids, and gases—have volume. If we want to measure matter, such as the fruit in **Figure 1**, we need to measure both mass and volume.

Weight First, consider weight. **Weight** is a measure of the force of gravity on an object. The force of gravity depends on the mass of the planet or moon where the object is being weighed. Because the moon has much less mass than Earth, on the moon you would weigh about one sixth of what you weigh on Earth. Jupiter has much more mass than Earth. On Jupiter, you would weigh more than twice what you weigh on Earth.

To find the weight of an object, you could place it on a scale like the ones shown in **Figure 2**. The object's weight pulls down on mechanisms inside the scale. These mechanisms cause beams or springs inside the scale to move. These movements are calibrated in such a way that the object's weight is displayed on the face of the scale.

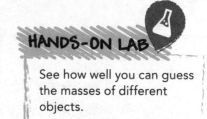

HANDS-ON LAB

See how well you can guess the masses of different objects.

Fruit Matter

Figure 1 At a fruit market, you can buy fruit by the pound. Pounds are a unit of weight.

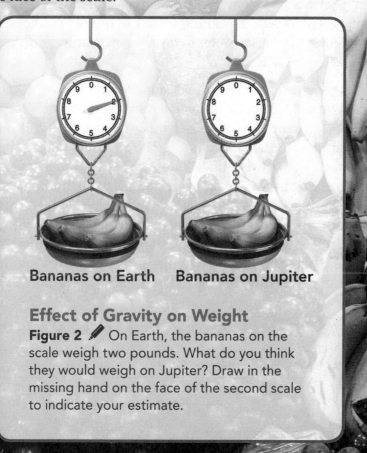

Bananas on Earth   **Bananas on Jupiter**

Effect of Gravity on Weight

Figure 2 ✏ On Earth, the bananas on the scale weigh two pounds. What do you think they would weigh on Jupiter? Draw in the missing hand on the face of the second scale to indicate your estimate.

Triple-Beam Balance Scale

Figure 3 A mechanical scale is like a see-saw. An object of unknown mass is put on one side of the scale, and then weighted tabs are moved on the other side of the fulcrum until the two sides are in balance. Gravity is acting on both sides with equal force, so it is not a factor in measuring mass this way.

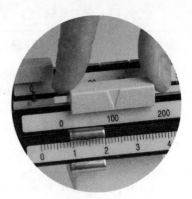

Mass Weight changes as the force of gravity changes. Even between different places on Earth, the force of gravity has slight variation, so your weight would as well. This means we need a measure of matter that is not affected by gravity. That's where mass comes in. Remember that mass does not change with location even if the force of gravity changes. For this reason, scientists prefer to describe matter in terms of mass rather than weight.

Scales that measure mass are designed to compare the known mass of an object to the unknown mass of another object (**Figure 3**). To measure mass, scientists use a system called the International System of Units (SI). The SI unit of mass is the kilogram (kg). In the United States, we tend to use pounds to measure weight. We can **convert** pounds to kilograms when the force of gravity at a location is known. If you weigh 130 pounds on Earth, your mass is about 60 kilograms, because a kilogram is equivalent to about 2.2 pounds. Sometimes, a smaller unit known as a gram (g) is used to measure mass. There are 1,000 grams in a kilogram, or 0.001 kilograms in a gram.

☑ READING CHECK **Summarize** What are weight, mass, and volume?

....

....

....

Volume Volume is the amount of space that matter takes up. We generally measure the volume of solids in the SI units of cubic meters (m^3), cubic centimeters (cm^3), or cubic millimeters (mm^3). We measure the volume of liquids in liters (L) and milliliters (mL). A milliliter is 1/1,000 of a liter and has the same volume as 1 cubic centimeter. Gases do not have a definite volume of their own because their particles move to fill their containers. So the volume of a gas is measured by the units of its container.

Math Toolbox

Calculating Volume

Objects of Regular Shape

The volume of an object of regular shape can be calculated by measuring the object's dimensions. For example, the volume of a boxlike piece of carry-on luggage that is 20 cm deep, 30 cm wide, and 45 cm long can be calculated by using this formula:
Volume = Length × Width × Height

1. **SEP Use Mathematics** What is the volume of the bag?

....

2. **SEP Use Mathematics** Large numbers can be rewritten by multiplying a number times a power of ten. For example, because 10^4 is equal to 10,000, you can rewrite 30,000 as 3×10^4. Rewrite your answer to Question 1 in this form.

....

Objects of Irregular Shape

One way to find the volume of an irregularly shaped object is by submerging it in a volume of water that is known. The volume of water that is displaced equals the volume of the object.

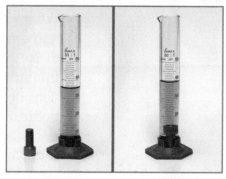

3. **SEP Design Solutions** Suppose the irregularly shaped object is a massive whale shark that is about to be moved into a cube-shaped aquarium tank. How might you combine the "Length × Width × Height" formula with the displacement method to determine the shark's volume? Explain.

....

....

....

....

....

....

Determining Density

A kilogram of sand takes up much less space than a kilogram of feathers. The volumes differ because sand and feathers have different densities—another important property of matter. **Density** is a measure of the mass of a material in a given volume.

Calculating Density Density can be expressed as the number of grams in one cubic centimeter (g/cm^3). For example, the density of water at room temperature is stated as "one gram per cubic centimeter" ($1 \ g/cm^3$). Recall that volume can also be measured in milliliters. So the density of water can also be expressed as $1 \ g/mL$. You can determine the density of a sample of matter by dividing its mass by its volume.

$$\text{Density} = \frac{\text{Mass}}{\text{Volume}}$$

When you drop things into bodies of water, some things sink and some things float. What determines this? You know the density of fresh water is $1 \ g/cm^3$. Objects with densities greater than that of water, such as a rock, will sink. Objects with lesser densities, such as a piece of wood, will float. If you shake a bottle of oil and vinegar, you will see the oil slowly separate to float above the vinegar. This happens because oil is less dense than vinegar.

Density and Water

Figure 4 When people throw coins into a fountain, the coins drop to the bottom. Why do the coins drop to the bottom of the fountain?

....

....

....

Model It

Liquid Layers

This beaker shows five layers of liquids of various densities. The liquids are listed in the table below.

Liquid	Density
vegetable oil	0.91 g/mL
honey	1.36 g/mL
corn syrup	1.33 g/mL
water	1.00 g/mL
dish soap	1.03 g/mL

SEP Develop Models ✏ Complete the model by using different shading for each layer shown, according to the densities in the table. Then, label each of the substances.

Density and Temperature You know that mass is a physical property. Density is a function of mass and volume, so it too is a physical property. Note that increasing or decreasing the total amount of a given substance won't change its density. If you have 5 or 75 cubic centimeters of silver, they will both have the same density because they are both made of the exact same substance.

One factor that does affect density is temperature. In general, most substances become less dense as temperature increases and more dense as temperature decreases. This is why warm masses of air rise up from Earth's surface and cold air masses sink toward Earth's surface. Water also follows this general rule, but not always. Liquid water does expand, or get less dense, when it gets warmer. It condenses, or gets denser, as it gets colder. But when water cools below 4°C, its density actually begins to decrease again, as you can see in the Math Toolbox.

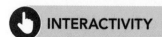
INTERACTIVITY

Investigate density using various materials including solid and liquid water.

HANDS-ON LAB

Investigate Explore the physical properties of mass, volume, and density.

Math Toolbox

Temperature and Density of Water

Although the density of water is usually considered to be 1 g/cm³, the true density of water varies with temperature, as shown in the table and graph.

1. **Claim** At what temperature is water densest? Circle that point on the graph and record your answer here.

   ....

2. **Evidence** Explain the sudden decrease in density when water is at 0°C as shown on the graph.

   ....

   ....

   ....

3. **Reasoning** If ice were, like most other substances, more dense than its liquid form, what would this mean for bodies of water that freeze in the winter? What would happen to the organisms that live in them?

   ....

   ....

   ....

   ....

   ....

| Density of Water vs. Temperature ||
Temperature (°C)	Density (g/cm³)
0 (ice)	0.9168
0 (water)	0.9998
4	1.0000
10	0.9997
25	0.9977

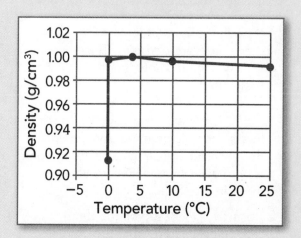

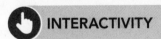
INTERACTIVITY

Compare the weights, masses, and densities of objects on Earth versus on the moon.

Using Density

Because density is an intrinsic property of matter, meaning that it does not change with the shape of an object, density can be used to identify substances. Imagine that you are looking for gold in stream beds in Alaska. You find an area where the gravelly streambed seems to be flecked with gold. First, you sort the gold-colored pieces from the other parts of the sediment. You set aside four of the largest pieces, hoping at least one of them will be valuable gold. You use a small digital scale and a graduated cylinder filled with water to measure the masses and volumes of each sample. Those data are shown below each sample in the Math Toolbox. If one of the samples has a density of 19.3 g/cm^3, then you've found gold!

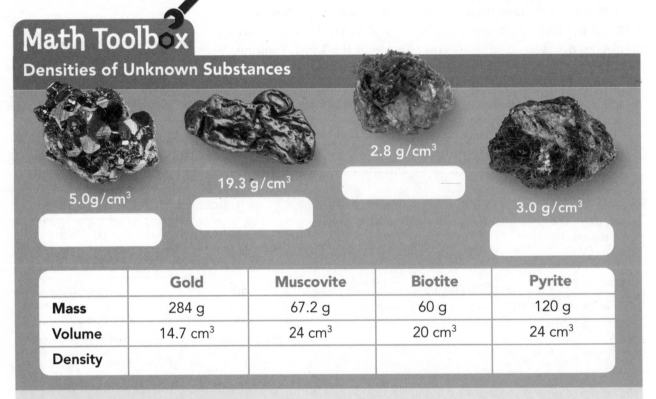

Math Toolbox

Densities of Unknown Substances

5.0g/cm^3

19.3 g/cm^3

2.8 g/cm^3

3.0 g/cm^3

	Gold	Muscovite	Biotite	Pyrite
Mass	284 g	67.2 g	60 g	120 g
Volume	14.7 cm^3	24 cm^3	20 cm^3	24 cm^3
Density				

Although these rocks look similar, they all have different densities. This physical property can help you determine which is really gold.

1. **SEP Use Mathematics** ✏ Use the mass and volume measurements given for each substance to calculate the density of each sample. Record your calculations in the table.

2. **Identify** ✏ Based on the densities you've calculated, write the correct names of the substances in the labels by the rocks.

3. **SEP Design Solutions** Besides density, what other physical property can you use to confirm that the gold is indeed real gold? Describe how you would conduct a test to confirm the sample's identity.

....

....

....

....

....

....

1. SEP Use Mathematics What is the mass of a sample of a substance with a volume of 120 mL and a density of 0.75 g/mL?

....

2. Explain If density usually increases with decreasing temperature, why does ice float on liquid water?

....

....

....

3. SEP Engage in Argument Why is mass a better unit for measuring matter than weight?

....

....

....

4. SEP Use Mathematics ✏ The force of gravity on the moon is only 16.6% the force of gravity on Earth. For each item listed in the table below, fill in what its weight would be on the moon.

Weights on Earth and the Moon		
Item	**Weight on Earth**	**Weight on the Moon**
Apple	150 g	
Hammer	1.5 lbs	
Person	180 lbs	
Blue whale	200 tons	

5. Use Mathematical Thinking A small bar of pure gold, whose density is 19.3 g/cm^3, displaces 80 cm^3 of water when dropped into a beaker. What is the mass of the bar of gold?

....

6. CCC Cause and Effect What might happen if a large cloud in the sky suddenly encountered a colder air mass with a temperature of 5°C?

....

....

....

....

7. SEP Engage in Argument In much of the world, SI units are used in everyday life and not just in science. Why would it make sense for people in the United States to use SI units in everyday life, too? Explain using math terms such as *calculate* and *convert*.

....

....

....

....

....

....

....

....

....

....

An EPIC DISASTER

On April 20, 2010, an explosion took place on an oil rig called Deepwater Horizon in the Gulf of Mexico. Within two days the rig had sunk to the ocean floor. Crude oil then leaked from the underwater oil well. The spill lasted 87 days and dumped millions of gallons of oil into the Gulf waters.

Because oil is less dense than water, it floats on the water's surface. The oil in the Gulf disaster, however, did not all float. Scientists estimate that about 10% of it sank to the sea floor. How could a less dense substance sink in a substance of higher density?

Three factors contributed to this phenomenon. First, some oil mixed with natural gas and seawater, causing it to become more dense. The second factor was the climate. Wind currents, ocean waves, and evaporation all acted on the oil and affected its density. The third factor was microorganisms called phytoplankton. They released a sticky substance when exposed to the oil. The substance stuck to bits of algae and other items, causing them to mix with oil and sink.

The Deepwater Horizon oil rig exploded in the Gulf of Mexico on April 20, 2010.

April

April 20 Deepwater Horizon oil rig explodes. 11 crew members are killed.

April 22 Oil rig sinks; oil slick appears on water's surface.

May

April 28 Coast Guard estimates that underwater well damaged in explosion is leaking oil into the Gulf.

210,000 gallons per day

May 4 Oil slick reaches Louisiana shores.

June

May 28 Attempt to pump mud into the well to block the oil fails.

Use the timeline to answer questions 1–2.

1. **SEP Use Mathematics** Approximately how much oil may have spilled into the water between April 20th and July 12th?

....

2. **SEP Construct Explanations** Why do you think it took so long for the workers to stop the flow of oil from the underground well?

....

....

3. **SEP Design Solutions** How might a team of engineers solve the problem of access to an underwater oil well for necessary repairs?

....

....

....

....

....

4. **Predict** What do you think the nations of the world should do to prevent disasters such as Deepwater Horizon from happening in the future?

....

....

....

July

August

July 5 Oil slick reaches Texas shores.

July 10 Broken containment cap is removed from well; oil now flows without any restrictions.

July 12 New containment cap is installed.

July 15 Oil has ceased to flow from the well.

August 5 The well is permanently sealed.

Guiding Questions

- How are changes in matter related to changes in energy?
- What is the difference between a physical change and a chemical change?

Connections

Literacy Write Explanatory Texts

Math Use Ratio Reasoning

MS-PS1-2

HANDS-ON LAB

uInvestigate Explore physical and chemical changes.

Vocabulary

physical change
chemical change

Academic Vocabulary

conservation

Connect It!

✏️ **Circle at least two things in the photo that are undergoing the process of changing matter.**

CCC Stability and Change What is causing the marshmallows to change their state of matter?

....

....

Form a Hypothesis Why do you think matter changes state when outside forces act upon it?

....

....

....

Physical Changes in Matter

A **physical change** alters the form or appearance of matter but does not turn any substance in the matter into a different substance. If you accidentally drop a glass onto a hard floor, the glass may shatter. However, the chemical composition of the broken glass is still the same. A substance that undergoes a physical change is still the same substance after the change.

Changes of State You have learned that most matter exists in three different states—solids, liquids, and gases. Suppose you leave an ice cube in a glass and forget about it. When you come back, there is a small amount of water in the glass. The ice cube has undergone a physical change. The solid water that made up the ice cube has melted into liquid water. A change in state, such as from a solid to a liquid or from a liquid to a gas, is an example of a physical change.

HANDS-ON LAB

Use chalk to distinguish between physical and chemical changes.

Reflect As you read this lesson, record examples of physical and chemical changes that you encounter, as well as examples that you think of from your own life. Categorize them in a two-column chart.

Changing States
Figure 1 Fire is a useful tool for causing changes in states of matter.

Sculpting Ice

Figure 2 An ice scultpor
breaks ice and shapes ice,
but he or she does not cause
it to change into another
substance.

Changes in Shape or Form

When you combine
two substances, how do you know if just a physical change
occurred or whether you have created an altogether new
substance? There are ways to figure it out. For example,
imagine that you pour a teaspoon of sugar into a glass of water
and stir until the sugar dissolves. If you pour the sugar solution
into a pan and boil away the water, the sugar will remain
as a crust at the bottom of the pan. The crust may not look
exactly like the sugar before you dissolved it, but it's still sugar.
Therefore, dissolving is a physical change.

Other examples of physical changes include bending, crush-
ing, breaking, and carving (**Figure 2**). Any change that alters
only the shape or form of matter is a physical change. Methods
of separating mixtures, such as filtration and distillation, also
involve physical changes.

☑ READING CHECK **Explain** How are melting and carving
ice sculptures both examples of physical changes?

....

....

....

....

Model It

Types of Physical Changes

✎ Make a paper airplane out of a piece of
scrap paper. Draw a sketch of your paper
airplane in the space provided.

1. **CCC Cause and Effect** What kinds
   of physical changes did you cause to
   happen to the paper?

   ....

2. **CCC Stability and Change** How can
   paper that has already been used be
   physically changed to make other paper
   products?

   ....

   ....

   ....

   ....

   ....

   ....

Chemical Changes in Matter

A change in matter that produces one or more new substances is a **chemical change**, or chemical reaction. In some chemical changes, a single substance breaks down into two or more other substances. For example, hydrogen peroxide breaks down into water and oxygen gas when it's poured on a cut on your skin. In other chemical changes, two or more substances combine to form different substances. Photosynthesis is a natural chemical change that occurs in plants and other photosynthetic organisms. Several compounds are combined using energy from the sun to produce new substances.

Some chemical changes can be initiated and observed in the kitchen. If you have ever baked bread with help from yeast, you have seen a chemical reaction at work. The yeast reacts with sugars in the mixture to produce bubbles of carbon dioxide, which make the dough rise (**Figure 3A**). Another chemical reaction takes place on the surface of the bread. As heat is added, the sugars turn into a brown crust (**Figure 3B**).

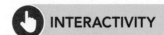

INTERACTIVITY

Investigate various properties of matter.

Chemical Change in the Kitchen

Figure 3 Adding yeast to dough causes a chemical change, which makes the dough rise.

Adding heat to the dough causes sugars to undergo a chemical change that results in a brown crust.

Tarnishing is the slow combination of a bright metal, such as silver, with sulfur or another substance, which produces a dark coating on the metal.

Oxidation is the combination of a substance with oxygen, such as when iron rusts.

Objects catch fire when a fuel combines rapidly with oxygen, producing heat, light, and new substances.

Bubbles are created by using electricity to break a compound down into elements or simpler compounds.

Types of Chemical Change

Figure 4 The images show different types of chemical changes. Next to each photo, identify the evidence that a new substance has formed.

Examples of Chemical Change One common chemical change is the burning of natural gas on a gas stove. Natural gas is mostly made up of the compound methane (CH_4). When it burns, methane combines with oxygen in the air and forms new substances. The new substances include carbon dioxide gas (CO_2) and water vapor (H_2O). Both of these substances can be identified by their properties, which are different from those of methane. **Figure 4** describes some of the types of chemical changes.

Conservation of Mass When something such as a piece of paper burns, it may seem to lose mass or disappear. Scientists, however, have proved that this is false. In the 1770s, the French chemist Antoine Lavoisier measured mass both before and after a chemical change. His data showed that no mass was lost or gained during the change. The fact that matter is not created or destroyed in any chemical or physical change is called the law of **conservation** of mass. This law is also called the law of conservation of matter because mass is a measurement of matter.

....

....

....

....

HANDS-ON LAB

🔲 **Investigate** Explore physical and chemical changes.

Math Toolbox

Conservation of Mass

The combustion reaction that produces carbon dioxide and water from methane and oxygen does not result in any gain or loss of mass. All atoms that go into the reaction are present at the end of the reaction.

| Methane molecule | Two oxygen molecules | Carbon dioxide molecule | Two water molecules |

| ☐ Carbon atom(s) | ☐ Hydrogen atom(s) | ☐ Oxygen atom(s) | | ☐ Carbon atom(s) | ☐ Hydrogen atom(s) | ☐ Oxygen atom(s) |

1. **SEP Use Models** 🖉 Count the atoms of each element before and after the chemical change. Fill in the numbers in the appropriate boxes.

2. **Use Ratio Reasoning** Does the ratio of hydrogen to oxygen change during the reaction? How do you know?

....

....

3. **SEP Ask Questions** Antoine Lavoisier was able to show that mass wasn't lost or gained during chemical reactions by weighing all of the matter in the system before and after reactions occurred. What questions would you ask Lavoisier about how he conducted his investigations?

....

....

....

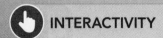
Energy and Matter Are Related

Do you have much energy for schoolwork today? In science, energy is the ability to do work or cause change. Any kind of change to matter involves a change in energy. Bending a paper clip or chopping an onion takes energy. When ice changes to liquid water, energy is absorbed from the matter around it.

Like matter, energy is conserved in a chemical change. Energy is never created or destroyed. It is only transformed.

Literacy Connection

Write Explanatory Texts How can you use terms such as *thermal energy*, *particles*, *motion*, and *flow* to explain the movement of heat in our world?

....

....

....

....

....

Temperature and Thermal Energy When you walk into a warm building on a cold winter day, you will immediately notice the difference between the cold outside and the warmth inside. We refer to the measure of how hot or cold something is as temperature. Temperature is related to the motion and energy of the particles of matter. The particles of gas in the cold outside air have less average energy of motion than the particles of air inside the warm building.

The total energy of the motion of all of the particles in an object is known as thermal energy. We usually talk about thermal energy in terms of how hot or cold something is, but thermal energy is not the same thing as temperature. Thermal energy naturally flows from warmer matter to cooler matter.

Movement of Thermal Energy

Figure 5 🖉 A polar bear swims in frigid waters of the Arctic, while people relax in a geothermal pool in Iceland. Draw arrows to indicate the direction that thermal energy moves in each image.

Thermal Energy and Changes in Matter

When matter changes, thermal energy is usually released or absorbed. For example, ice absorbs thermal energy from its surroundings when it melts, leaving the air around it feeling cold. That's why coolers for food and drinks are filled with ice. The melting of ice is an endothermic change, or a change in which energy is absorbed. An exothermic change occurs when energy is released. Combustion is an exothermic change.

Chemical energy is stored in the chemical bonds between atoms. Foods, fuels, and even the cells in your body store chemicals. Burning fuels transforms chemical energy and releases some of it as thermal energy. When you ride a bike up a hill, chemical energy from food changes into the energy of your muscles's motion, which your legs convert into mechanical energy through the bike's pedals.

Obtaining Chemical Energy

Figure 6 When this giraffe consumes food, the chemical reactions that occur during digestion are a source of energy for the giraffe.

Math Toolbox

Energy in Chemical Reactions

A student initiates two chemical reactions by adding a different substance to each of two beakers with different solutions. She observes them for 10 minutes, recording the temperature of the solution in each beaker every minute.

1. **SEP Use Mathematics** What was the temperature change of each solution after 10 minutes?

   ....

   ....

2. **SEP Interpret Data** Which of the beakers had an endothermic reaction? Which had an exothermic reaction

   ....

   ....

3. **SEP Communicate Information** Which solution could be used in a cooling pack to keep food and drinks cold in a cooler? Explain.

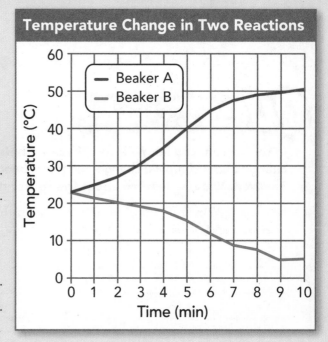

Temperature Change in Two Reactions

....

....

31

1. Classify A large bar of solid gold is melted into liquid. The liquid is then poured into molds to make a number of gold coins. Was this a chemical or physical change? Explain.

....

....

....

2. Infer If you cut an apple into slices and leave them in the open air, they will slowly turn brown. What kind of chemical change is this? Explain.

....

....

....

3. SEP Engage in Argument A friend notices that a nail that was left outside for a few months seems larger and heavier than it was before. He says it disproves the law of conservation of mass. Explain why he is wrong.

....

....

....

....

4. SEP Construct Explanations A northern right whale migrates from warm waters off Florida to cooler waters off Nova Scotia, Canada. In which area do you think more thermal energy would move from the whale to its environment? Explain.

....

....

....

....

....

....

5. Summarize A stick of butter is melted in a saucepan. As it continues to cook, the butter turns brown. What changes have occurred?

....

....

....

....

....

....

Quest CHECK-INS

In this lesson, you learned the difference between a physical change and a chemical change and how changes in energy are involved. You also learned about the conservation of mass.

Evaluate Why is it important to know the difference between chemical and physical changes when designing special effects?

....

....

....

....

....

INTERACTIVITY

Mysterious Movie Fog

HANDS-ON LAB

Cinematic Science

Go online to learn how "dry ice" and other substances are used to make physical and chemical changes in special effects.

MS-PS1-2

Gathering Speed with SUPERCONDUCTORS

VIDEO

Find out about maglev trains and how they work.

The maglev train flashes past in a blur! If you blink, you might miss it. Maglev trains carry passengers at speeds of more than 370 miles per hour.

The Challenge: To use superconductivity to make a fast, efficient train.

Phenomenon "Maglev" is short for "magnetic levitation." A maglev train doesn't run on tracks; it floats just above them. Magnetic principles elevate the train, propel it forward, and keep it on its correct route. The magnets rely on a physical property called superconductivity.

In superconductivity, a substance loses all electrical resistance when it is cooled to a certain temperature (usually below −253°C or −423°F). At these low temperatures, certain elements and alloys become not just good conductors of electricity, but superconductors. This transition from a conductor to a superconductor is an important physical change! Once a metal is superconducting, it can generate incredibly strong magnetic fields—strong enough to elevate a train!

In the case of the maglev train, mercury is the superconductor. For the magnetic field of a maglev train to be strong enough to drive the train, the electromagnets must be cooled to a very cold −267°C!

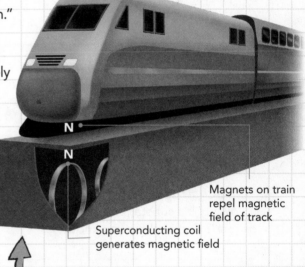

N
N

Magnets on train repel magnetic field of track

Superconducting coil generates magnetic field

Maglev trains operate on the simple principle of magnetic attraction and repulsion. The surface below a magnet is cooled enough to become superconducting, allowing the magnet to levitate.

DESIGN CHALLENGE

Can you use magnets to build a model of a maglev train? Go to the Engineering Design Notebook to find out!

33

1 Describing and Classifying Matter

MS-PS1-1

1. Which of the following changes demonstrates a chemical property?
   A. substance breaks in half
   B. substance combusts
   C. hammer bounces off substance
   D. substance floats in water

2. Which of the following is a solution?
   A. salt water
   B. macaroni and cheese
   C. cake mix
   D. vegetable soup

3. The abilities to dissolve in water and to conduct electricity are examples of
   A. natural properties.
   B. chemical properties.
   C. natural laws of matter.
   D. physical properties.

4. SEP Construct Explanations Which of the following is a substance: table salt, seawater, or sand? Explain how you know.

....

....

....

....

....

....

....

2 Measuring Matter

MS-PS1-2

5. Which is the correct equation for calculating density?
   A. Density = Mass/Volume
   B. Density = Mass/Weight
   C. Density = Volume/Mass
   D. Density = Volume/Weight

6. What is the density of an object whose mass is 180 grams and whose volume is 45 cm^3?
   A. 4 cm^3/g   **B.** 0.25 g/cm^3
   C. 4 g/cm^3 **D.** 0.25 cm^3/g

7. Weight is a flawed measure of mass because it
   A. is not used in other countries.
   B. is affected by the force of gravity.
   C. tends to fluctuate.
   D. can be influenced by temperature and pressure.

8. SEP Design Solutions Describe two ways to measure the volume of a solid object.

....

....

....

....

....

....

....

....

....

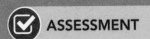
3 Changes in Matter

MS-PS1-2

9. Which of the following describes a physical change?

A. A marshmallow burns over an open flame.

B. Icicles melt from a rooftop.

C. A cat eats a piece of fish.

D. Milk turns sour.

10. Which of the following describes a chemical change?

A. clear liquids mix, producing a cloudy liquid with yellow chunks

B. silver coins are melted down and shaped into a solid brick

C. salt is added to a pot of hot water, and the water's boiling point changes

D. an apple is chopped into eight slices

11. The law of conservation of mass states that

A. matter is neither created nor destroyed.

B. the mass of an object remains the same even if chemical change occurs.

C. the number of molecules before and after a chemical reaction cannot change.

D. mass is lost when a chemical change occurs.

12. Temperature is

A. the movement of thermal energy from a solid to a liquid.

B. the difference in thermal energy between two objects.

C. a measure of how hot or cold something is.

D. a measure of how fast thermal energy is moving.

13. ....and..............................
are two types of energy that can be released when something burns.

14. **SEP Interpret Data** Look at the image of a salad with chicken on a countertop. In which direction is thermal energy moving? Cite evidence to support your answer.

....

....

....

....

....

....

....

....

....

....

MS-PS1-1

Evidence-Based Assessment

A group of students is developing models of simple molecules to help them describe and classify matter. The materials they have are pipe cleaners along with red, blue, and yellow clay.

The students are modeling four molecules. The data for these molecules is presented in the chart below.

Hydrogen	Hydrogen chloride	Ammonia	Nitrogen trichloride
2 Hydrogen atoms	1 Hydrogen atom	1 Nitrogen atom	1 Nitrogen atom
	1 Chlorine atom	3 Hydrogen atoms	3 Chlorine atoms

The students' models of the first three molecules are shown, with one of the models constructed incorrectly.

1. **SEP Analyze Data** Based on the data and the first two models, which atom is represented by the red clay?

A. Nitrogen   B. Hydrogen
C. Chlorine   D. Oxygen

2. **SEP Use Models** Which of the following can be done using the students' models? Select all that apply.

A. Visualize the atoms bonded within the molecules

B. Determine the thermal energy of a hydrogen chloride atom

C. Show that some molecules are not compounds

D. Demonstrate how elements can combine to form different types of matter

3. **Determine Differences** How does the hydrogen molecule differ from the other molecules?

....

....

....

....

....

4. **SEP Define Problems** Which model has been constructed incorrectly? Explain how you would fix it.

....

....

....

....

....

....

5. **SEP Construct Explanations** Review the chart to determine which atoms are needed to model nitrogen trichloride. Describe how you would build the model, including which colors of clay you would use.

....

....

....

....

....

Quest FINDINGS

Complete the Quest!

Phenomenon Determine the best way to clearly present your ideas for the movie scene and the special effects that you would propose to the film director. You may present the storyboards or run through the actual scene as though it were being filmed.

Optimize Your Solution Are there any safety considerations or other issues that you encountered when demonstrating or discussing your special effects? How would they influence a redesign of your proposal?

....

....

....

....

....

....

....

INTERACTIVITY

Reflect on Your Movie Scene

Help Out the Wildlife

How can you **separate** a **mixture** into its pure **substances**?

Background

Phenomenon Overnight, a materials storage facility was struck by an intense hurricane. The winds destroyed the building, and the rains washed salt, sand, and iron filings into a nearby pond. You wake up to a phone call from the Department of Environmental Protection asking if you can help to clean up the contamination. Wildlife are at risk in the murky water. The owner of the storage facility also would like to recover as much salt, sand, and iron filings as possible. They should not go to waste!

Your job is to design a procedure to remove the salt, sand, and iron filings from the water.

Materials

(per group)

- 60-g mixture of salt, sand, and iron filings
- assorted materials and tools to separate the mixture

Safety

Be sure to follow all safety procedures provided by your teacher.

Murky Waters
Contaminated water can be a threat to the health of wildlife.

Sand, Salt, and Iron Filings

Plan Your Investigation

1. Your teacher will divide the class into groups and provide each group with a mixture of water, salt, sand, and iron filings to model the flooding. Your mixture will contain the same quantities as other groups so that you can compare results.

2. Design a plan to remove the sand, salt, and iron from the water and separate them from each other. You may want to consider some of these questions as you design your plan:

   - What materials can you use to fully separate the sand, iron, and salt?

   - Are there other substances you can use to help you separate the mixture?

   - What steps can you take to maximize the amount of each substance you recover from the mixture?

3. Identify the materials you will need to separate the sand, iron, and salt from the mixture. Record your materials in the space provided below.

4. Develop your plan by creating a procedure. Record your procedure, paying careful attention to the order of the steps.

5. Finally, draw a data table in which you can record the mass of each substance that you recover and the material(s) that you used to do it.

HANDS-ON LAB

☐ **Demonstrate** Go online for a downloadable worksheet of this lab.

Materials

Procedure

....
....
....
....
....
....
....
....
....
....
....
....
....

Data Table

Analyze and Interpret Data

1. **SEP Evaluate Information** Compare your results with another group. What were the similarities and differences in your findings?

....

....

....

....

....

2. **CCC Cause and Effect** What may be the causes of the differences in the masses recovered by each group?

....

....

....

....

....

3. **Apply Scientific Reasoning** If you started with dry sand, salt, and iron filings, how would you change your procedure? Would any order work?

....

....

....

....

....

4. **SEP Design Solutions** Review the procedure and results of another group. If you were able to do the lab over again, what specific things would you do differently?

....

....

....

....

....

....

Solids, Liquids, and Gases

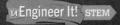
NGSS PERFORMANCE EXPECTATION

MS-PS1-4 Develop a model that predicts and describes changes in particle motion, temperature, and state of a pure substance when thermal energy is added or removed.

Why can you see this horse's breath in the cold?

HANDS-ON LAB

uConnect See if you can identify all the states of matter in three bottles.

GO ONLINE
to access your
digital course

 VIDEO

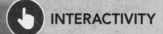 INTERACTIVITY

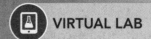 VIRTUAL LAB

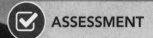 ASSESSMENT

 eTEXT

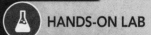 HANDS-ON LAB

The Essential Question

What causes matter to change from one state to another?

SEP Construct Explanations You can see a cloud of your breath outside on a cold day but not on a warm day. What do you think is happening to your breath in the cold air?

....

....

....

....

....

....

Quest KICKOFF

How can you use solids, liquids, and gases to lift a car?

STEM **Phenomenon** Auto mechanics often need to go under cars to repair the parts in the under-carriage, such as the shocks and exhaust system. It's much easier for them to do their job if they have more room to work, so they use lift systems to raise the cars overhead. In this problem-based Quest activity, you will design an elevator or lift system that uses a solid, liquid, or gas to raise a model car. You will explore the properties of solids, liquids, and gases to see how they can be used in a lift mechanism. You will investigate how potential changes of state affect or impose constraints on your design. By applying what you have learned through lessons, digital activities, and hands-on labs, you will design, build, test, and evaluate a model elevator or lift.

NBC LEARN ▶ VIDEO

After watching the Quest Kickoff video, which examines different ways that elevators and lifts work, write down what you already know about solids, liquids, and gases.

Solids:

....

....

Liquids:

....

....

Gases:

....

....

INTERACTIVITY

Getting a Lift

MS-PS1-4 Develop a model that predicts and describes changes in particle motion, temperature, and state of a pure substance when thermal energy is added or removed.

Quest CHECK-IN

IN LESSON 1

STEM What are the properties of solids, liquids, and gases? Think about how you can use those properties in your lift device.

INTERACTIVITY

Design Your Lift

Quest CHECK-IN

IN LESSON 2

STEM How might a change in state affect a process? Consider how changes in the state of matter might affect your lift. Then develop a final design.

INTERACTIVITY

Lift Your Car

Auto mechanics raise cars above their heads to repair parts such as engines and transmission systems.

Quest CHECK-IN

IN LESSON 3

STEM What criteria and constraints affect your model? Build and test your lift device. Improve and retest as needed.

HANDS-ON LAB

Phases of Matter

Quest FINDINGS

Complete the Quest!

Demonstrate your lift and evaluate its performance. Reflect on your work and consider other applications for your device.

👆 **INTERACTIVITY**

Reflect on Your Lift

Solid, Liquid, or Gas?

Background

Phenomenon Imagine that your little sister's class is studying matter. She asks you if all the kinds of matter in bottles are liquids. To help her understand the answer, you decide to show her examples of different states of matter that can be put in a bottle.

> How can you **develop and use models** to illustrate examples of the different states of matter?

Develop Models

1. **SEP Develop Models** Describe how you will use the materials to make three models. Remember, you need to show materials in each state of matter. You can show more than one state in a bottle or a single state of matter in a bottle but you need to show each state of matter. See if you can get one bottle to show all three states.

   ....

   ....

   ....

   ....

2. Show your plan to your teacher for approval, and then assemble your bottles. Observe the matter inside each bottle.

3. In the observation section, draw a table and record your observations.

Materials

(per group)
- 3 clear plastic bottles with lids
- water
- ice
- seltzer
- marbles
- paper towels
- funnel (optional)

Safety

Be sure to follow all safety procedures provided by your teacher. The Safety Appendix of your textbook provides more details about the safety icons.

Observations

HANDS-ON LAB

🔲**Connect** Go online for a downloadable worksheet of this lab.

Analyze and Interpret Data

1. **CCC Patterns** Use your observations to explain each state of matter.

   ....

   ....

   ....

   ....

   ....

2. **CCC Cause and Effect** Explain how and why the states of matter in any of the bottles might change if they sit out for an hour.

   ....

   ....

   ....

3. **SEP Use Models** What other materials could fill the bottles and be used as examples of liquids, solids, and gases?

   ....

   ....

   ....

4. **SEP Construct Explanations** Should your sister conclude that all kinds of matter in bottles are or are not liquids? Use your observations to support your answer.

   ....

   ....

① States of Matter

Guiding Questions

- What are the similarities and differences between solids, liquids and gases?
- What is the relationship between particle motion and state of matter?

Connection

Literacy Write Informative Texts

MS-PS1-4

HANDS-ON LAB

uInvestigate Distinguish between states of matter by understanding their properties.

Vocabulary

solid
liquid
surface tension
viscosity
gas

Academic Vocabulary

vibrate

Connect It !

✏️ **How many solids, liquids, and gases can you find in this picture? Label the solids with an S, liquids with an L, and gases with a G.**

SEP Construct Explanations During winter, you can sometimes ice skate outdoors on a frozen lake. Why can't you ice skate on a lake when it is not frozen?

....

....

....

Solids, Liquids, and Gases

Everything around you is made of matter. Matter exists in different forms, depending on a variety of factors, such as temperature.

Suppose you are taking a walk around a lake on a snowy day, such as in **Figure 1**. Everywhere you look, water is around you in different forms. It crunches loudly as snow beneath your feet. Liquid water on the surface of the lake flows freely when the wind blows. And invisible water particles exist in the air you breathe. The water around you is in three different phases of matter: solid, liquid, and gas.

HANDS-ON LAB

☑**Investigate** Distinguish between states of matter by understanding their properties.

Literacy Connection

Write Informative Texts Describe a solid, liquid, and gas found outdoors where you live.

....

....

....

....

....

Water Everywhere
Figure 1 Water exists in different forms on Earth.

Describing Solids

The ring box in **Figure 2** contains a ring made of pure silver. What would happen if you took the ring out of the box and placed it on your finger? Would it drip onto the floor? Of course not, because it's a solid. A **solid** has a definite shape and a definite volume. Remember that volume is the amount of space that matter fills. Volume is usually measured in cubic centimeters (cm^3), cubic meters (m^3), milliliters (mL), or liters (L).

A book is another example of a solid. If you place a book in your backpack, it will stay the same shape and size as it was before. A solid maintains its shape and volume in any position or container.

Academic Vocabulary

Strings on a guitar vibrate to create sound waves that make music. Why does a cell phone vibrate?

....

....

....

....

Particles of a Solid
The particles that make up a solid are packed very closely together, as shown in **Figure 2**. This fixed, closely-packed arrangement of particles causes a solid to have a definite shape and volume. The particles in a solid are closely locked in position such that they cannot move around one another on their own. They can only **vibrate** in place, meaning they move back and forth slightly (see **Figure 3**).

A Ring of Solid Silver
Figure 2 The solid ring has a definite shape and volume.

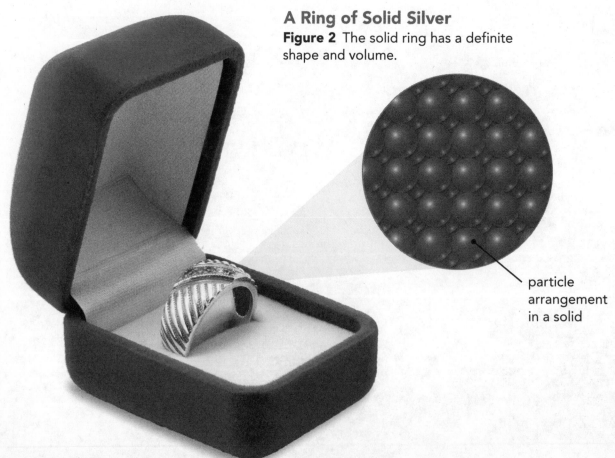

particle
arrangement
in a solid

Dancing In The Crowd
Figure 3 People at a packed concert don't move very far, but if they're having fun, they're not standing still either! These people dancing in place are a lot like particles vibrating in a solid.

SEP Communicate Information Think about the motion of the particles in a solid and come up with your own way of describing them.

....

....

....

....

....

Physical Properties of Solids Of course, not all solids are the same. Some are hard and brittle, while some are flexible. Some have smooth surfaces and are heavy, while others are sharp and light. Take a look at the natural quartz and the eraser in **Figure 4**. These are both solids, but they are very different!

Comparing Solids
Figure 4 Determine Differences
Write down the differences that you notice in shape, structure, and texture between the quartz and the eraser.

Eraser
....
....
....

Quartz
....
....
....

Types of Solids The particles inside quartz are aligned in a regular, repeating pattern. This pattern creates crystals. Solids that are made up of crystals are called crystalline solids. Salt, sugar, and snow are examples of crystalline solids. When a crystalline solid is heated, it melts at a distinct temperature.

On the other hand, the material that makes up an eraser is an amorphous solid. In amorphous solids, such as the butter shown in **Figure 5**, the particles are not arranged in a regular pattern. Also, an amorphous solid does not melt at a distinct temperature. Glass is an example of an amorphous solid. It might look crystalline when it is cut into nice shapes, but it is amorphous because of its particle arrangement and the fact that it does not melt at a specific temperature. A glass blower can bend and shape glass that has been heated because it gradually becomes softer. Rubber and plastics are other examples of amorphous solids. They are very useful in manufacturing because they can be gradually heated and cooled to take specific, detailed shapes such as shoe soles and toys.

Model It!

Crystalline and Amorphous Solids

Figure 5 🖊 A pat of butter is an amorphous solid. The particles that make up the butter are not arranged in a regular pattern. The sapphire gem stones are crystalline solids. Draw what you think the particles look like in a crystalline solid.

☑ **READING CHECK** **Explain** In your own words, explain the main differences between crystalline solids and amorphous solids.

....
....
....
....
....
....
....

Describing Liquids

What happens when you spill a drink? It spreads into a wide, shallow puddle as shown in **Figure 6**. Without a container, your drink does not have a definite shape. Like a solid, however, it does have a constant volume. Drinks such as water, cranberry juice, and iced tea are liquids. A **liquid** has a definite volume but no shape of its own.

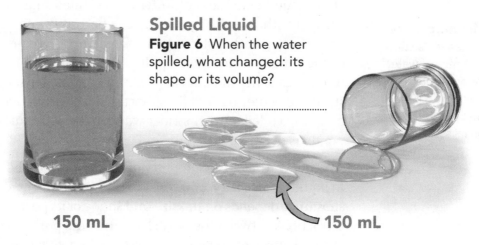

Spilled Liquid
Figure 6 When the water spilled, what changed: its shape or its volume?

....

150 mL   **150 mL**

Particles of a Liquid In general, the particles in a liquid are always in contact with one another. They are packed almost as closely together as those in a solid. However, the particles in a liquid are not fixed in place. They can move around one another. You can compare this movement to the way you might move a group of marbles around in your hand. Like the particles of a liquid, the marbles slide around one another but still touch. These freely moving particles allow a liquid to flow from place to place. For this reason, a liquid is also called a fluid, meaning a "substance that flows." Because its particles are free to move, a liquid has no definite shape. However, it does have a definite volume, as shown in **Figure 7**.

Liquids Change Shape
Figure 7 These two pools hold the same volume of water even though they have different shapes. Liquids take the shape of their containers.

particle arrangement in a liquid

51

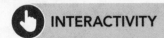
INTERACTIVITY

Identify the arrangement and motion of particles in solids, liquids, and gases.

Make Meaning Have you ever seen leaves sitting on top of the surface of water? In your science notebook, describe the property of the liquid water that allows the leaves to sit on its surface.

Physical Properties of Liquids

Substances can be classified by their characteristic properties—physical or chemical properties that remain the same no matter how large or small the sample. Two major characteristic properties of liquids are surface tension and viscosity.

Surface tension is an inward force, or pull, among the molecules in a liquid that brings the molecules on the surface closer together. A glass of water can be filled slightly above the rim without spilling over. That's because water molecules attract one another strongly. These attractions cause molecules at the water's surface to be pulled slightly toward the water molecules beneath its surface. Due to surface tension, the surface of water can act like a sort of skin. Surface tension lets an insect called a water strider walk on the calm surface of a pond, as in **Figure 8**.

Another characteristic property of matter that can be observed in liquids is **viscosity**, or a resistance to flowing. The viscosity of a substance depends on the size and shape of its particles and the attractions between the particles. When the particles are larger or more attracted to one another, they do not flow as freely. Liquids with high viscosities flow slowly. Honey is an example of a liquid with a very high viscosity (**Figure 9**). Liquids with low viscosity flow quickly. Water and vinegar have relatively low viscosities. Substances in other states of matter have viscosity as well. For example, solids have higher viscosity than liquids.

☑ **READING CHECK** **Write Informative Texts** Would honey be considered more viscous or less viscous than cranberry juice? Why?

....

....

....

Surface Tension

Figure 8 Does this water strider have magic powers? Not quite. Because of surface tension, the water strider is able to do the impossible: walk on water.

Viscous Honey

Figure 9 Honey flows slowly compared to many other liquids.

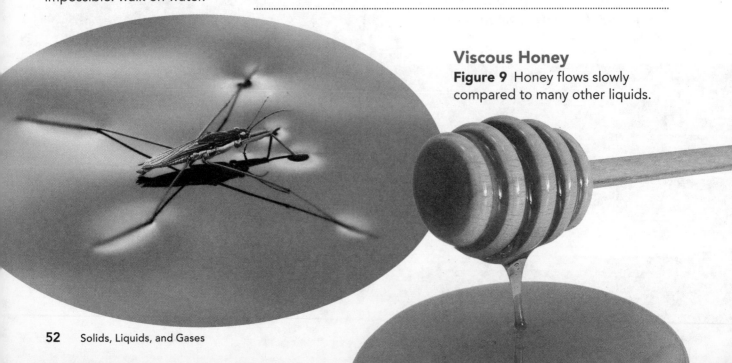

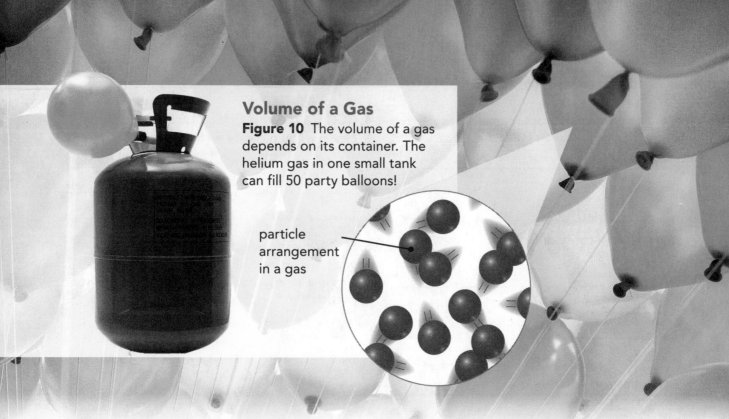

Volume of a Gas

Figure 10 The volume of a gas depends on its container. The helium gas in one small tank can fill 50 party balloons!

particle arrangement in a gas

Describing Gases

Like a liquid, a gas is a fluid. It has particles that can move around one another. However, unlike a liquid, a **gas** has neither a definite shape nor a definite volume. That's because the particles in a gas do not remain in contact with one another.

Particles of a Gas If you could see the particles that make up a gas, you would see them moving in all directions. They are widely spaced and collide with one another as they fly about. When a gas is in a closed container, the gas particles move and spread apart to fill the container.

Physical Properties of Gases Because gas particles move and fill all of the space available, the volume of a gas is the same as the volume of its container. For example, a large amount of helium gas can be compressed—or pressed together tightly—to fit into a metal tank. When you use the helium to fill balloons, it expands to fill many balloons that have a total volume much greater than the volume of the tank, as in **Figure 10**. In general, the particles of a gas flow more easily than the particles of a liquid, so gases have lower viscosity than liquids.

✓ **READING CHECK** **Determine Central Ideas** What are the main differences between gases and liquids?

....

....

....

▶ VIDEO

Discover the fourth state of matter: plasma!

👆 INTERACTIVITY

Use what you have learned to identify states of matter and describe their particles.

MS-PS1-4

1. Identify What two properties of a gas depend on its container?

....

....

2. Determine Differences How do liquids with a high viscosity differ from liquids with a low viscosity?

....

....

....

3. CCC Energy and Matter What are the similarities and differences of the particle motion in solids and liquids?

....

....

....

....

....

....

4. CCC Cause and Effect How do the particles in a liquid create surface tension?

....

....

....

5. SEP Develop Models ✏ Based on what you have learned, draw models of the particles in a solid, a liquid, and a gas. Use dots for particles and arrows to show motion.

Solid   **Liquid**

Gas

Quest CHECK-IN

You have learned about the characteristics of solids, liquids, and gases. You discovered the differences in particle motion for these states of matter as well.

CCC Energy and Matter How can you use the different states of matter to your advantage when designing a device that lifts a car? What different solids, liquids, and/or gases might you use in your design?

....

....

....

....

....

👆 **INTERACTIVITY**

Design Your Lift

Go online to review properties of solids, liquids, and gases. Then brainstorm ideas and begin your plans for a device that could lift a car.

MS-PS1-4

From "Ink" to Objects: 3D PRINTING

When you hear the word *printing*, you probably think of words and images on paper. But 3D printing has little to do with books!

The Challenge: To utilize the properties of solids and liquids to make 3D objects.

Phenomenon Have you heard of 3D printing? Unlike traditional printing, which simply binds ink onto paper or other media, 3D printing makes physical shapes that have mass and volume. How do these printers work?

Remember what you have learned about solids and liquids. In liquids, particles can move and slide past one another, while in solids, particles are fixed in place and only vibrate. This gives liquids and solids their unique properties. However, these properties can be changed by applying energy, such as heat.

Think of what happens when you melt butter. You take the butter, which is a solid, and apply heat, melting the butter into a new form—a liquid. 3D printers work in the same way. They take a solid material, usually a plastic or a metal, and apply heat until the material melts into a liquid. Then, the liquid is sprayed or squeezed onto a platform, according to a design that has been programmed into the printer. The liquid material hardens again into a solid. After many layers build up, a 3D object is completed.

3D printers can make complex 3D objects quickly and easily. They are useful to a wide variety of production industries!

DESIGN CHALLENGE What could you design with a 3D printer? Go to the Engineering Design Notebook to find out!

② Changes of State

Guiding Questions

- How does thermal energy play a role in particle motion and changes of state?
- What happens to particles during changes of state between solids, liquids, and gases?
- How does pressure affect the change of state from liquid to gas?

Connections

Literacy Use Information

Math Draw Comparative Inferences

MS-PS1-4

HANDS-ON LAB

uInvestigate Understand why fog can sometimes form on a mirror.

Vocabulary

thermal energy
temperature
melting point
freezing point
vaporization
boiling point
evaporation
condensation
sublimation

Academic Vocabulary

suspend

Connect It !

🖊 If you've ever watched a burning candle, you've seen how the solid wax melts into a liquid. Circle an area in the picture where you see this happening.

CCC Stability and Change When the liquid wax cools, it hardens. How is wax hardening similar to liquid water turning to ice?

....

....

....

Thermal Energy and Temperature

You have seen substances change state. For example, snow melts into liquid water, puddles of rain freeze in the cold, and boiling water becomes steam. What do all of these changes have in common? They involve a change in the thermal energy and temperature of the substance. Thermal energy and temperature are related, but they are not the same thing. You can understand them in terms of particles.

Thermal Energy Particles have both kinetic energy and potential energy. Kinetic energy is energy of motion, and potential energy is energy that is stored. **Thermal energy** is the total kinetic and potential energy of all the particles in an object or substance.

You can increase the thermal energy of a substance by heating it. When you apply heat, you are transferring energy from the heat source to the substance. If you add enough energy to the substance, it can become hot enough to change its state of matter, like the candle wax in **Figure 1**.

Temperature Recall that all particles of matter are constantly moving. **Temperature** is a measure of the average kinetic energy of the particles in an object or substance. The faster the particles are moving, the greater their kinetic energy and the higher the temperature of the substance.

A thermometer measures temperature in degrees, such as degrees Celsius (°C) or degrees Fahrenheit (°F). The thermometer registers a higher temperature when particles are moving faster. How do you make particles speed up? Heat a substance, such as the cider in **Figure 2**, so that its thermal energy increases and its particles move faster. As a result, the temperature of the substance will increase. On the other hand, when a substance is cooled and its thermal energy decreases, its particles slow down. The temperature of the substance decreases.

Hot Apple Cider
Figure 2 Apple cider is best served hot!

☑ **READING CHECK**
Integrate With Visuals
✐ Draw an arrow on **Figure 2** to show the direction of heat flow. Label the apple cider's thermal energy as increasing or decreasing.

Dripping Candles
Figure 1 The candle wax experiences a change of state as it melts.

INTERACTIVITY

Examine how particles move and how temperature changes when thermal energy increases or decreases.

Changes of State Between Solid and Liquid

Have you ever let a bar of chocolate sit in a car too long on a hot day? If so, you know what it looks like when the chocolate melts. Some of the solid bar changes to liquid.

Melting When the temperature of most solids increases enough, the solids change to liquid. The change in state from a solid to a liquid is called melting. This change of state involves an increase in thermal energy. In general, particles of a liquid have more thermal energy than particles of the same substance in solid form.

In pure, crystalline solids, melting occurs at a specific temperature, called the **melting point**. **Figure 3** shows what happens to the temperature of an ice cube after it is taken from the freezer and left out at room temperature. At first, the energy flowing from the environment into the ice makes the water molecules vibrate faster, raising the temperature of the ice cube. At a solid's melting point, its particles vibrate so fast that they break free from their fixed positions. When the ice cube reaches the melting point of water, 0°C, its temperature stops increasing. At this point, added energy continues to change the arrangement of the water molecules from ice crystals into liquid water as the ice melts.

Write About It Have you ever eaten an ice cream cone on a hot summer day? What happened to the ice cream? Think about cause and effect, and write about what happened in your science notebook.

Changing Ice Into Water

Figure 3 The graph shows approximately how the temperature of solid ice changes as it melts into liquid water.

SEP Interpret Data How long did it take for the ice to completely melt once it reached the melting point?

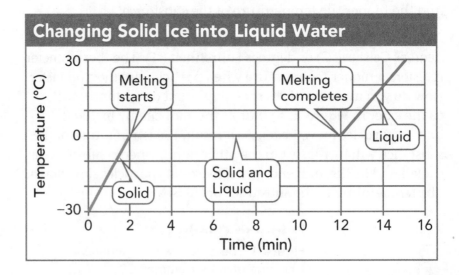

Changing Solid Ice into Liquid Water

Because the melting point is a characteristic property of a substance, chemists often compare melting points when trying to identify an unknown material. For example, silver and iron are both shiny metals with a similar color. The melting point of silver is 961.8°C, while the melting point of iron is 1,538°C. No matter how much of a substance there is, it will always melt at the same temperature.

Freezing You have probably seen many substances freeze. When you put liquid water into a freezer, for example, it turns to solid ice. The thermal energy of the liquid water decreases and the water molecules move more slowly. At 0°C, the water molecules begin to become fixed in place, and the liquid water turns to solid ice.

Freezing is the change of state from a liquid to a solid. It is the reverse of melting. Unlike water, some substances do not have to be cold to the touch in order to freeze. For example, some types of wax freeze at 63°C, which is greater than the record high surface temperature of Earth ever recorded. A substance's **freezing point** is simply the temperature at which it changes from a liquid to a solid. So, water's freezing point is 0°C, and the special wax's freezing point is 63°C. At a liquid's freezing point, its particles are moving so slowly that they begin to take on fixed positions. It doesn't matter how much of a substance there is—it will always have the same freezing point.

☑ READING CHECK **Determine Central Ideas** What is the difference between melting and freezing?

....

....

....

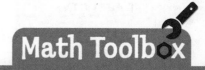

Math Toolbox

The Freezing Point

The graph shows a substance changing from liquid to solid.

1. SEP Interpret Data Based on the graph, what is the value of the freezing point for this substance?

....

2. Draw Comparative Inferences Think about what would happen if this substance were in the solid phase first, then melted into a liquid. What can you say about the solid's melting point compared to the liquid's freezing point?

....

....

....

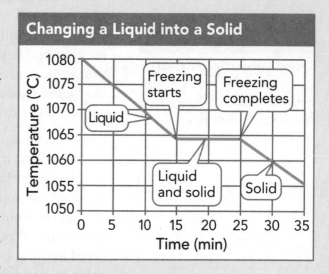

Changing a Liquid into a Solid

3. Identify ✏ The following are four substances and their melting points. Which substance does the graph represent? Circle your answer.

Platinum: 1768.3°C   Gold: 1064.18°C   Silver: 961.78°C   Mercury: −38.83°C

Evaporation or Boiling?

Figure 4 Examples of vaporization are all around us.

Identify Label each picture as boiling, evaporation, or both.

INTERACTIVITY

Observe and describe the motion of particles in substances at different temperatures.

Literacy Connection

Use Information Based on the information given, write down the main differences between boiling and evaporation.

....

....

....

....

....

....

....

Changes of State Between Liquid and Gas

Why does a pot of hot soup create steam? How does fog form? To answer these questions, you need to look at what happens when changes occur between the liquid and gas states.

Evaporation and Boiling The change in state from a liquid to a gas is called **vaporization** (vay puhr ih ZAY shun). Vaporization occurs when the particles in a liquid gain enough energy to move independently and away from each other. There are two main types of vaporization—boiling and evaporation.

Vaporization that takes place both below and at the surface of a liquid is called boiling. When soup boils, vaporized soup molecules form bubbles below the surface. The bubbles rise and eventually break the surface of the liquid, as shown in **Figure 4**. The temperature at which a liquid boils is called its **boiling point**. The boiling point of water is 100°C at sea level. As with melting and freezing points, boiling points are characteristic properties and can be used to identify unknown substances. No matter how much of a substance you have, it will boil at the same temperature.

You know that a rain puddle eventually disappears from the ground as it changes from a liquid to a gas. The puddle of water vaporizes, but why don't we see the water boiling? Because the temperature of the water in the puddle has not reached its boiling point, only the water particles on the surface of the puddle have enough energy to turn into a gas. Energy is transferred to these particles from the sun's radiation and the surrounding air. Vaporization that takes place only on the surface of a liquid is called **evaporation**. The process continues until all of the particles evaporate and the puddle is gone. While boiling occurs only at one temperature, evaporation can occur at all temperatures.

The Effect of Pressure

When you push on an object, you apply pressure to the object. The pressure depends on the force you apply and the area over which you apply the force.

$$\text{Pressure} = \text{Force} / \text{Area}$$

Gas particles constantly collide with one another and with any nearby surfaces. As a result, a gas pushes on these surfaces. The pressure a gas applies is greater if its particles collide with a surface more often, as shown in **Figure 5**.

The air that surrounds you is constantly applying pressure to you. This pressure, called atmospheric pressure, can affect how easily a liquid changes to a gas. Think about boiling water to make pasta. Atmospheric pressure is acting on the surface of the liquid water. As the water is heated on the stove, the pressure inside of the liquid increases. When the pressure inside of the liquid equals the atmospheric pressure, the liquid boils.

In locations high above sea level—such as Denver, Colorado—the atmospheric pressure is less because the air is less dense. This means that it takes less thermal energy to get a liquid to boil in these locations. In Denver, water boils at 95°C.

▶ VIDEO

Discover how planes form vapor trails in the sky.

Pressure and Vaporization

Figure 5 ✎ Circle the image in which the liquid would require more thermal energy to change to a gas. How did you determine your answer?

....

....

....

....

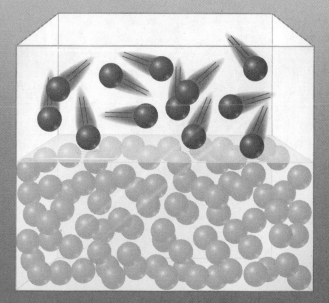

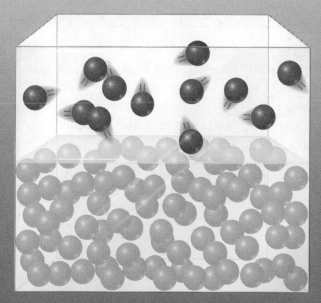

HANDS-ON LAB

☑ **Investigate** Understand why fog can sometimes form on a mirror.

Academic Vocabulary

In orange juice, bits of pulp are suspended in liquid. Explain what you think *suspended* means.

....

....

....

....

....

Condensation

The reverse of vaporization is condensation. **Condensation** is the change in state from a gas to a liquid. It occurs when particles in a gas lose enough thermal energy to change state.

You can observe condensation by breathing onto a window, as shown in **Figure 6**. When warm water vapor in your breath reaches the cooler surface of the window, the water vapor condenses into liquid droplets.

Have you ever wondered how fog forms? Much like clouds in the atmosphere, fog forms (**Figure 7**) when water vapor in the air condenses into tiny liquid droplets. Water vapor is a colorless gas that you cannot see. The steam you see above a kettle of boiling water is not water vapor, and neither are clouds or fog. What you see in those cases are tiny droplets of liquid water **suspended** in air.

Condensation on a Window

Figure 6 Warm breath condenses on the cool surface of a window.

Foggy Mountains

Figure 7 Fog forms in the cool air.

☑ **READING CHECK** **Draw Evidence** What is happening to the water vapor in the air in this photograph?

....

....

....

Changing State from Solid to Gas

☝ **INTERACTIVITY**

Draw conclusions about how thermal energy affects particle motion, temperature, and state.

In places where the winters are very cold, the snow may disappear even when the temperature stays well below freezing. This change is the result of sublimation. **Sublimation** occurs when the surface particles of a solid gain enough energy that they form a gas. During sublimation, particles of a solid do not pass through the liquid state as they form a gas.

One example of sublimation occurs with dry ice, which is solid carbon dioxide. At ordinary atmospheric pressures, carbon dioxide cannot exist as a liquid. So instead of melting, solid carbon dioxide changes directly into a gas as shown in **Figure 8**. As it sublimes, the carbon dioxide absorbs thermal energy from its surroundings. For this reason, dry ice can be used to keep materials cold. Some fog machines use dry ice to create fog in movies. When dry ice becomes a gas, it cools water vapor in the nearby air. The water vapor then condenses into a liquid, forming fog near the dry ice.

Model It !

Dry Ice

Figure 8 Dry ice sublimes, changing directly from a solid to a gas.

SEP Develop Models ✏ Think about what is happening to the particles of carbon dioxide as the dry ice changes from solid to gas. Draw models of the particles in the two phases of matter. Use an arrow to show the flow of thermal energy into the solid carbon dioxide.

1. CCC Cause and Effect What is the main cause of any change of state?

....

....

....

2. SEP Construct Explanations If there is high gas pressure above a liquid, what can you say about the amount of thermal energy required for the liquid to change to gas?

....

....

....

3. Compare and Contrast In terms of changes in particle motion and thermal energy, how does condensation differ from evaporation?

....

....

....

....

....

....

4. Predict If you left a block of dry ice in a bowl at room temperature all day, what would happen to it?

....

....

....

....

....

5. CCC Energy and Matter Solid substance A has a melting point of 100°C. Liquid substance B has a freezing point of 110°C. For each substance, identify its state of matter and describe the motion of its particles when the substance is at 115°C.

....

....

....

....

....

....

....

Quest CHECK-IN

In this lesson, you learned what happens to the particles of substances during melting, freezing, evaporation, boiling, condensation, and sublimation. You also thought about how thermal energy plays a role in these changes of state.

SEP Define Problems Why do you need to take the temperature of the surroundings into consideration when designing a system with materials that can change state?

....

....

....

....

👆 **INTERACTIVITY**

Lift Your Car

Go online to use your knowledge of changes of state to identify the benefits and drawbacks of different ideas for your design.

MS-PS1-4

FREEZE that Scalpel!

How do refrigerators and freezers keep food from spoiling? They circulate chilled air. The cold temperatures prevent bacteria from forming.

Cryosurgery works in a similar way. It uses extremely cold temperatures to treat cancers, pre-cancerous growths, warts, moles, and skin infections.

While refrigerators and freezers use freon to keep food cold, cryosurgery generally uses liquid nitrogen to freeze unwanted, harmful cells. At room temperature, nitrogen is a colorless, odorless gas. However, when it undergoes extreme cold, it condenses into a liquid. To achieve this state, the nitrogen has to be cooled to around −200°C! At this temperature, liquid nitrogen instantly freezes anything it touches, and with human tissue, it can destroy cells upon contact. After treatment, the dead cells and tumors thaw and are absorbed harmlessly into the system. If the tumor is on the skin's surface, a scab forms and eventually drops away.

Cryosurgery is very new in the field of medicine, and new techniques are being developed every day. For example, some doctors have started using liquefied argon gas, rather than liquid nitrogen, because it allows for even faster freezing of cells. Doctors and scientists are also exploring ways to use cryosurgery safely to target cells from the inside out, instead of from the outside in.

MY DISCOVERY

Type "cryosurgery" into an online search engine to learn more about this technology and the conditions it can treat.

Liquid nitrogen freeze technique treats a skin cancer.

Skin lesion

Liquid nitrogen

Cryosurgery is used to kill tumors that could not be reached and cut out.

3 Gas Behavior

Guiding Questions

- How do changes in particle motion of a gas affect physical properties?
- How are the temperature, pressure, and volume of a gas related?

Connections

Literacy Read and Comprehend

Math Graph Proportional Relationships

MS-PS1-4

Vocabulary

pressure
Charles's Law
Boyle's Law

Academic Vocabulary

proportional

Connect It !

When a volleyball sits out in the sun, it becomes warmer and feels more firm.

Apply Concepts What do you think happens to the particles of air inside the ball as it warms in the sun?

....

....

SEP Construct Explanations What do you think happens to a volleyball outside on a cold night?

....

....

....

Pressure and Temperature of a Gas

Have you ever shaken a snow globe? If so, you've seen how the fake snowflakes fly around. They collide with each other and with the walls of the snow globe. If you shake it more slowly, the snowflakes collide less frequently.

Gas particles in a container are a lot like the snowflakes in a snow globe. The gas particles constantly collide with one another and with any walls that may contain them. As a result, a gas pushes against the walls of its container. The **pressure** of a gas is the force of its outward push (in Newtons) over an area (in square meters) of the walls of the container. Pressure is measured in units of pascals (Pa) or kilopascals (kPa) (1 kPa = 1,000 Pa).

The pressure of a gas can affect the physical properties of an object. For example, the volleyball in **Figure 1** feels firm when the pressure of the air inside of the ball is greater than the pressure of the air outside of the ball. Because the air particles inside of the ball are tightly packed, there are more frequent collisions with its inner surface. This results in a higher pressure.

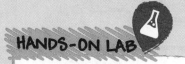

HANDS-ON LAB

Discover how bubble wrap can prevent chalk from breaking.

Volleyball in the Sun
Figure 1 The air pressure inside a volleyball increases as it warms in the sun.

Pressure in a Basketball

Figure 2 When a basketball leaks air, the pressure inside decreases. It loses its bounciness and becomes "flat."

CCC Cause and Effect
✎ On each image, write a physical property that changes due to low gas pressure in the object.

If you get a tiny hole in a pumped-up ball, air will slowly leak out, as shown in **Figure 2**. Because the pressure inside the ball is greater than the outside air, the interior gas particles hit the inside of the ball more often. Gas particles inside the ball exit more often than gas particles outside of the ball enter. As a result, the pressure inside the ball drops until it is equal to the pressure outside.

Temperature also affects the pressure of a gas. When you heat a gas, its particles move faster, so the temperature increases. The particles will collide with the walls of their container with greater force and more frequency. A greater force over the same area results in greater pressure.

In general, when the temperature of a gas at constant volume is increased, the pressure of the gas increases. When the temperature is decreased while volume is constant, the pressure of the gas decreases.

Literacy Connection

Read and Comprehend
As you read, underline the sentences that explain the motion of particles as a gas is heated.

✅ READING CHECK **Summarize** How does particle motion affect pressure?

....

....

Temperature and Volume

French scientist Jacques Charles examined the relationship between the temperature and volume of a gas. He measured the volume of a gas at various temperatures in a container that could change volume. Because the volume was able to change, the pressure remained fairly constant.

HANDS-ON LAB

Investigate Test Charles's and Boyle's Laws.

Charles's Law Charles discovered that when the temperature of a gas at constant pressure is increased, its volume increases. He also discovered that when the temperature of a gas at constant pressure is decreased, its volume decreases. This principle is called **Charles's law**.

Figure 3 shows Charles's Law in action. A balloon is slowly lowered into liquid nitrogen at nearly –200°C and then removed. In the process, the pressure remains more or less constant.

Cooling and Warming a Balloon

Figure 3 🖊 The volume of a gas-filled balloon changes as the temperature changes. Below each image, shade the arrows to indicate whether temperature and volume increase or decrease at each step.

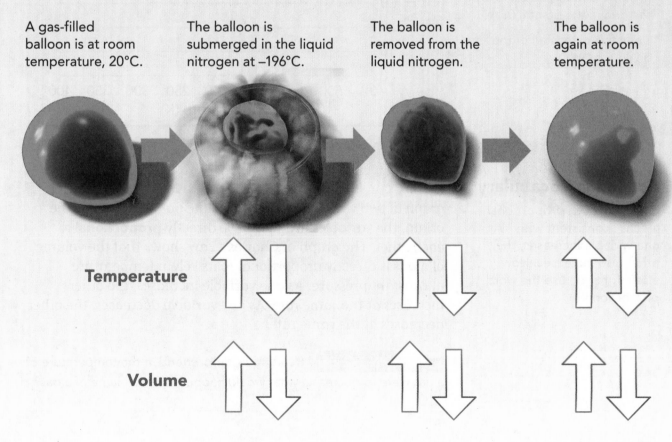

A gas-filled balloon is at room temperature, 20°C.

The balloon is submerged in the liquid nitrogen at –196°C.

The balloon is removed from the liquid nitrogen.

The balloon is again at room temperature.

Temperature

Volume

69

Graphing Charles's Law

Suppose that you do an experiment to test Charles's law. The experiment begins with 50 mL of gas in a container that can expand. The gas is slowly heated. Each time the temperature increases by 20°C, the gas volume is recorded. The data are recorded in the data table. Note that the temperatures in the data table have been converted to kelvins, the SI unit of temperature. To convert from degrees Celsius to kelvins (K), you simply add 273.

Temperature		Volume
(°C)	(K)	(mL)
0	273	50
20	293	54
40	313	58
60	333	62
80	353	66

Graph Proportional Relationships ✏ Plot the data from the table on the graph.

As you can see from your graph, the data points form a straight line. If you extended the line, it would pass through the origin (the point 0,0).

Draw this extension of the line on your graph.

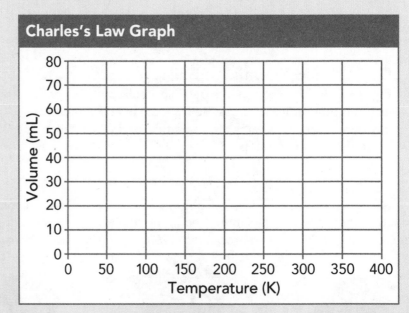

Charles's Law Graph

Academic Vocabulary

In this context, *proportional* means "consistent with." As one variable increases, the other also increases. How else might you use the word *proportional*?

....

....

....

....

Directly Proportional Relationships When a graph of two variables is a straight line passing through the origin, the variables are said to be directly **proportional** to each other. The graph of Charles's Law shows that the volume of a gas is directly proportional to its kelvin temperature at constant pressure. As one variable increases, the other increases at the same rate. As one variable decreases, the other decreases at the same rate.

✓ READING CHECK **Read and Comprehend** If the temperature of a gas were to decrease, what would happen to the volume of a gas?

....

Pressure and Volume

Suppose that you use a bicycle pump to inflate a tire, as shown in **Figure 4**. By pressing down on the plunger, you force the gas inside the pump through the rubber tube and out of the nozzle into the tire. What happens to the volume of air inside the pump cylinder as you push down on the plunger? What happens to the pressure?

Boyle's Law In the 1600s, the scientist Robert Boyle carried out experiments to try to improve air pumps. He measured the volumes of gases at different pressures. Boyle's experiments showed that gas volume and pressure were related.

When the pressure of a gas at constant temperature is increased, the volume of the gas decreases. When the pressure is decreased, the volume increases. This relationship between the pressure and the volume of a gas is called **Boyle's Law**. Boyle's Law describes situations in which the volume of a gas is changed. The pressure changes in the opposite way. For example, as the handle of a bike pump is pressed, it pushes the particles downward in the cylinder. The volume in the cylinder becomes smaller, and particles leave through the tube.

INTERACTIVITY

Watch an animation to understand Charles's Law and Boyle's Law.

Filling a Bike Tire
Figure 4 Pumping a bike pump causes an increase in gas pressure and a decrease in gas volume within the pump.

Model It

SEP Develop Models Draw two diagrams to show the air particles in a bike pump before and after the handle is pushed down.

Air in pump before handle is pushed

Air in pump after handle is pushed

Math Toolbox

Graphing Boyle's Law

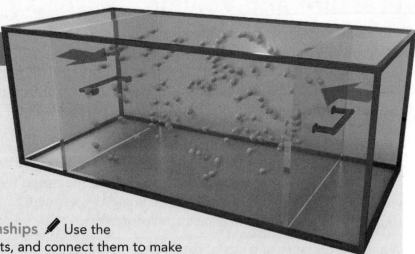

In an experiment, the volume of a gas was varied at a constant temperature. The pressure of the gas was recorded after each 50-mL change in volume. The data are shown in the table.

1. Graph Proportional Relationships ✏ Use the data from the table to plot points, and connect them to make a line graph.

2. Claim What happens to the pressure of a gas when the volume is decreased at a constant temperature?

....

3. Evidence Choose two points on the graph. For each point, multiply the pressure and the volume. How do these two products compare?

....

4. Reasoning Is the relationship between pressure and volume directly proportional, as in Charles's Law? Explain.

....

....

....

Volume (mL)	Pressure (kPa)
300	20
250	24
200	30
150	40
100	60
50	120

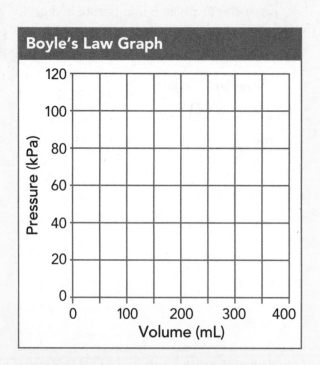

Boyle's Law Graph

Inversely Proportional Relationships Look at the graph that you made when graphing Boyle's Law in the Math Toolbox. Notice that the points lie on a curve and not a straight line. This curved line is called a hyperbola. When volume is low, pressure is high. When pressure is high, volume is low. As the volume of a gas increases at constant temperature, the pressure of the gas decreases at a different rate. If you multiply the two variables—pressure and volume—at any point on the curve, you will find that the product does not change. This means that the two variables are inversely proportional to each other. The graph for Boyle's Law shows that gas pressure is inversely proportional to volume at constant temperature.

Real-World Gas Behavior Pistons are often used in machines in which gas is involved. Pistons move in response to the motion of the particles of gas. For example, pistons in a car engine respond to pressure changes that occur when a mixture of fuel and air ignites. The moving pistons help to turn the crankshaft, which connects to the wheels of the car. So the pistons drive the turning of the wheels, which allows the car to move.

VIDEO

Go online to see how a car engine works.

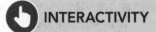
INTERACTIVITY

Explore how a hot-air balloon uses relationships between pressure, volume, and temperature.

Pistons in an Engine
Figure 5 Pistons in car engines move up and down. This drives the turning of the wheels of the car.

How Pistons Work

Figure 6 Use what you have learned about gas behavior to understand how temperature, pressure, and volume affect pistons.

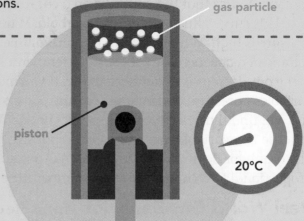

gas particle

Temperature and Pressure

The image shows gas particles above a piston in a rigid container. The piston is held fixed.

Relate Change ✎ Finish this sentence by circling the correct answer: If the temperature of the gas increases, the pressure on the piston will

(increase / decrease).

piston

20°C

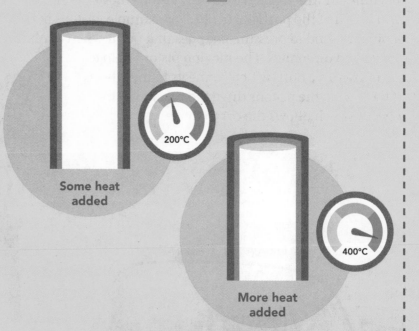

Temperature and Volume

Now, the piston is free to move up or down. Heat is applied to the gas in the cylinder.

Apply Scientific Reasoning
✎ Finish this sentence by circling the correct answer: As temperature increases, the volume of the gas will

(increase / decrease).

SEP Develop Models ✎ In each cylinder, draw the piston and the gas particles based on the temperature shown.

200°C

Some heat added

400°C

More heat added

Pressure and Volume

This time, the gas is kept at a fixed temperature. The piston is pushed by an outside force, so the pressure on the gas increases.

Integrate With Visuals What happens to the volume of the gas as the pressure increases?

....

....

SEP Develop Models ✎ Under the cylinders, rank the pressure from lowest to highest with 1 being lowest and 3 being highest. Rank the volume from lowest to highest as well.

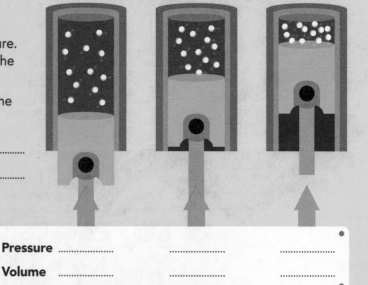

Pressure ....

Volume ....

1. SEP Construct Explanations What relationship does Charles's Law explain?

....

....

....

2. Identify If the gas pressure in a ball is low, how will it affect the physical properties of the ball?

....

....

....

3. CCC Cause and Effect When the temperature of a gas increases, and volume is fixed, what happens to the gas pressure? Why?

....

....

....

....

....

....

4. Synthesize Information How do particles of gas move when there is high temperature and high pressure?

....

....

....

5. CCC Stability and Change Environmental scientists collect air samples so they can test the quality of the air. They start with rigid metal containers that are completely empty—the air has been pumped out of them. What happens to the pressure inside the container and the volume of the container as air enters it?

....

....

....

....

....

Quest CHECK-IN

You learned about the relationships between the temperature, pressure, and volume of a gas. You also modeled how the gas particles behave in different situations.

SEP Design Solutions Using the relationships you have learned about between temperature, pressure, and volume, what are two ways you could increase the gas pressure of a system?

....

....

....

....

....

HANDS-ON LAB

Phases of Matter

Go online to download the worksheet of this lab. Build and test your device. Redesign and retest the device as needed.

RISING to the OCCASION:
Charles's Law in the Oven!

Have you ever baked bread or rolls? If so, you probably observed that during baking, the bread rises, increasing in volume. What causes this to happen? The answer lies in chemistry.

In the heat of an oven, gas bubbles in bread dough expand, causing the bread to rise.

Chemistry in Baking

Chemistry and baking go together naturally. In fact, chemistry affects every aspect of preparing food. The ingredients in a recipe may react with one another during the mixing process. Then, when you add heat—whether from a stove, a conventional oven, or a microwave oven—another whole set of reactions may occur. Charles's Law rules the effect of heat on food.

As you have read, Charles's Law states that temperature affects the volume of a gas. Assuming constant pressure, gas expands as temperature rises.

When a chef mixes ingredients, the dry ingredients absorb the wet ingredients. In baking, the dry ingredients usually include either baking powder or baking soda. And when baking bread, the most important dry ingredient is yeast. All three of these dry ingredients react with wet ingredients, such as milk or water, by creating tiny bubbles of carbon dioxide gas. Therefore, the dough that goes into the oven is filled with gas bubbles. The oven's heat makes these bubbles expand, forcing the dough to rise. The texture within the dough then becomes more sponge-like, with tiny holes and cavities created by the expanding bubbles of carbon dioxide gas.

Getting dough to rise properly can be a tricky task! When yeast is used, temperature affects the state of the dough before it even goes into the oven. Yeast is very active around 30°C. Putting the dough in a refrigerator, and thereby lowering the temperature around it, slows down the reaction that produces gas bubbles. Bakers need to have a good understanding of how temperature will affect their ingredients at every stage of the baking process to make sure their baked goods come out just right. In some recipes and under some conditions, bread may rise—increase in volume— by as much as 33 percent in the oven!

1. **Identify Patterns** What pattern does Charles's Law suggest about recipes with ingredients that might produce gas during cooking?

   ....

   ....

2. **Construct Explanations** Study the 3D image of a bread dough sample on the right. Explain what you see in the image, and describe the process that happens to dough in a hot oven. Use evidence to support your explanation.

   ....

   ....

   ....

3. **Predict** What would probably happen if you tried to bake bread without using yeast? Why?

   ....

   ....

4. **Refine Your Plan** Suppose you are mixing ingredients for bread, and the recipe says to bake the dough as soon as it's mixed. But, you have another task to do and are unable to bake the dough right away. What should you do to make sure your bread still turns out well?

   ....

   ....

5. **Calculate** If a baker gets the most rise out of his bread, what will be the volume of a loaf of bread that started out as a 30-cm^3 lump of dough?

   ....

1 States of Matter

MS-PS1-4

1. A substance that has neither a definite shape nor a definite volume is a
A. fluid.   **B.** solid.
C. liquid.   **D.** gas.

2. In a solid, particles do not move around each other, but they do
A. change shape.   **B.** vibrate.
C. flow.   **D.** sit completely still.

3. Sugar is considered a crystalline solid because its particles are
A. arranged in a regular pattern.
B. arranged randomly.
C. completely motionless.
D. able to move around one another.

4. CCC Energy and Matter How is a gas different from a liquid?

....

....

....

....

5. SEP Communicate Information ✐ Use the Venn diagram to compare and contrast the characteristics of solids and liquids.

Solid   Both   Liquid

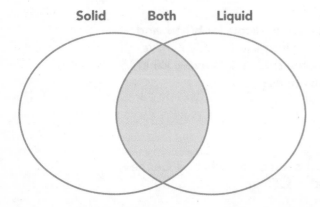

2 Changes of State

MS-PS1-4

6. Vaporization that takes place both above and below the surface is called
A. evaporation.   **B.** boiling.
C. condensation.   **D.** precipitation.

7. When a liquid freezes into a solid, the particles of the substance
A. lose energy.   **B.** gain energy.
C. move faster.   **D.** disappear.

8. Label each image as evaporation, boiling, condensation, or sublimation. Write more than one answer for an image if you notice more than one change of state.

....

....

....

....

....

....

9. When the gas pressure above a liquid increases, the amount of thermal energy required for the liquid to vaporize

....

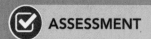
10. The melting point of aluminum is 660°C. At what temperature will aluminum melt if you have 5 grams? 10 grams? Explain your answer.

....
....
....
....
....

11. **SEP Develop Models** ✏ Make a diagram with two drawings showing the particle motion of a substance in two states as it condenses. Use arrows on the first drawing to show the direction thermal energy is moving.

State of Matter: ....

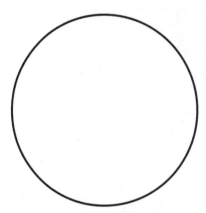

State of Matter: ....

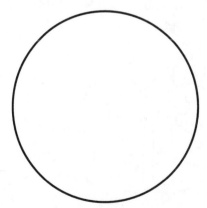

3 **Gas Behavior**

MS-PS1-4

12. When the temperature of a gas decreases, and volume is held constant, the pressure of the gas
A. stays the same. **B.** increases.
C. becomes zero. **D.** decreases.

13. Adding thermal energy to a gas at constant pressure will cause
A. the volume of the gas to decrease.
B. the volume of the gas to increase.
C. the temperature of the gas to decrease.
D. the pressure of the gas to decrease.

14. **SEP Interpret Data** Does this graph represent a directly or inversely proportional relationship? Explain what this means for the relationship between pressure and volume.

....
....
....
....

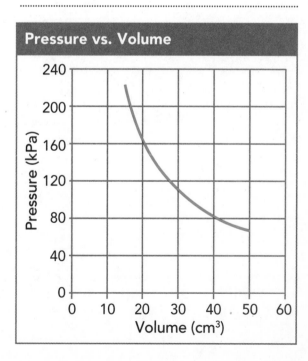

Pressure vs. Volume

MS-PS1-4

Evidence-Based Assessment

On a sunny morning, Skyler's father fills his new swimming pool with water from a garden hose. The following day, he notices that the water level has dropped—there is less water in the pool than there was the day before. He checks the pool for any leaks, but he finds nothing.

Skyler has a hunch as to why the water level has dropped. He draws some models to help explain what has happened.

Model 1:

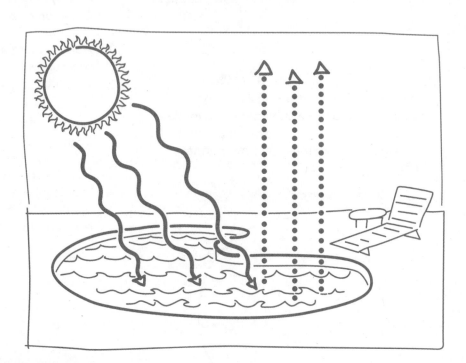

Model 2:

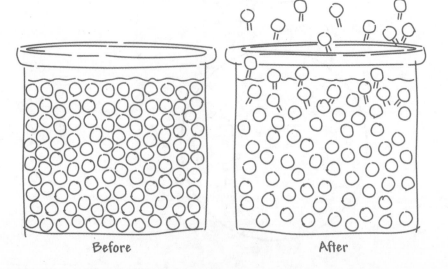

Before   After

1. **Identify** What change of state is Skyler representing with his models?
   A. condensation   **B.** evaporation
   C. sublimation   **D.** melting

2. **SEP Use Models** Look at Model 1. What do the lines from the sun to the water represent? What do the dotted lines coming from the surface of the water represent?

   ....

   ....

   ....

   ....

   ....

   ....

3. **SEP Develop Models** What labels and/ or drawings would you add to Model 1 to improve it?

   ....

   ....

   ....

   ....

   ....

   ....

4. **Cite Evidence** Describe what is happening to the thermal energy of the water in the pool during the day. Use evidence from the models to explain your answer.

   ....

   ....

   ....

   ....

   ....

   ....

   ....

   ....

5. **Draw Comparative Inferences** Look at Model 2. What two states of matter are shown in the "After" picture? Support your answer with evidence from the model. What is happening to the kinetic energy of the water molecules at the surface? What does this imply about the temperature of the water?

   ....

   ....

   ....

   ....

   ....

   ....

   ....

   ....

Quest FINDINGS

Complete the Quest!

Phenomenon Determine the best way to present your device to your class. Think about the ways you could improve upon your device.

CCC Scale, Proportion, and Quantity Think of a situation in which you might need to lift a real car. Describe the situation below. If your device could be made on a larger scale, how might it work in the situation?

....

....

....

....

👆 **INTERACTIVITY**

Reflect on Your Lift

MS-PS1-4

Melting ICE

Can you develop a **model** to predict and describe how **temperature** affects the particles of a raft made of ice?

Background

Phenomenon Off the coast of Alaska, your ship has sunk, but you manage to survive by climbing on an iceberg. You need a raft to float to the mainland. The only things available are floes, which are sheets of ice. The liquid water temperature is warmer than the ice, so your raft is going to melt as you travel!

In this investigation, you will use two ice cubes to explore how the temperature of liquid water affects how quickly ice melts. Gather evidence to conclude how long an ice raft will last in two cases: where the liquid water temperature is 40–45°C, and where the liquid water temperature is 20–25°C.

Materials

(per group)

- stopwatch or timer
- thermometer
- 2 plastic cups
- 2 plastic spoons
- 2 ice cubes, about 2 cm on each side
- warm water, 40–45°C
- room-temperature water, 20–25°C

Safety

Follow all safety guidelines provided by your teacher.

Design an Investigation

1. Begin by making a prediction about the results of the experiment using your background knowledge of ice. Include how long you think it will take each ice cube to melt completely into a liquid. Apply your prediction to your ice raft situation: assuming the mainland is far enough away that it would take 5 minutes for you to float there, would your raft stay solid long enough in 40–45°C water? How about in 20–25°C water?

....

....

....

....

HANDS-ON LAB

*u***Demonstrate** Go online for a downloadable worksheet of this lab.

2. Next, design, develop, and conduct an experiment to test your prediction. Use the space below to sketch, and the next page to write, your procedure. Think about these questions when designing your experiment.

- How might the size of the ice cubes affect your results?

- Will the amount of water in each cup affect your results?

- Would the motion of the ice cube affect your results?

- How might you move the ice cube to model the raft's motion?

- What factors will be controls in your experiment?

3. In addition to writing your procedure, design a data table to record your observations and measurements. Be sure to use the correct metric units in your data table.

4. Tell your teacher your hypothesis and describe your procedure. Once your procedure is approved, run your experiment and record your results in the data table.

Procedure

....
....
....
....
....
....
....
....
....
....
....
....
....

Data Table

Analyze and Interpret Data

1. Predict Were your predictions about the ice cubes supported by the results of the experiment? Explain why or why not.

....

....

....

2. SEP Interpret Data In which cup did the liquid water temperature change the most? Discuss your results.

....

....

....

....

3. SEP Construct Explanations When the ice melted, its particles gained enough energy to overcome the forces holding them together as solid ice. What was the source of that energy?

....

....

4. Identify Limitations In what ways did the experiment accurately reflect icebergs melting in ocean water? In what ways did the experiment simplify the real-word scenario?

....

....

....

5. SEP Develop Models In the space provided, draw two models or diagrams to show the arrangement of particles in the ice before and after thermal energy was added. For each model, identify the temperature and the state of matter.

SEP.1, SEP.8

The Meaning of Science

Science Skills

Reflect Think about a time you misplaced something and could not find it. Write a sentence defining the problem. What science skills could you use to solve the problem? Explain how you would use at least three of the skills in the table.

Science is a way of learning about the natural world. It involves asking questions, making predictions, and collecting information to see if the answer is right or wrong.

The table lists some of the skills that scientists use. You use some of these skills every day. For example, you may observe and evaluate your lunch options before choosing what to eat.

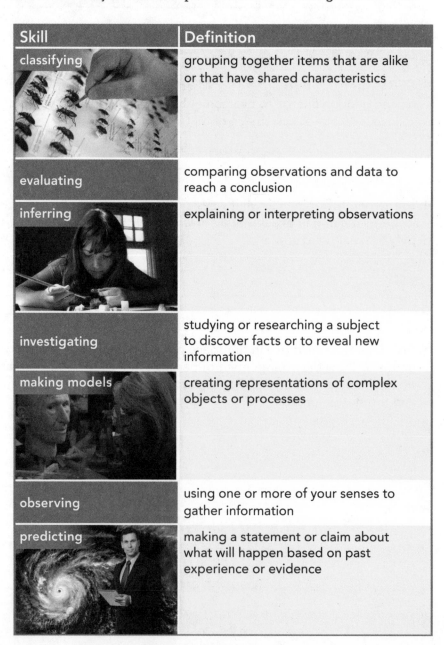

Skill	Definition
classifying	grouping together items that are alike or that have shared characteristics
evaluating	comparing observations and data to reach a conclusion
inferring	explaining or interpreting observations
investigating	studying or researching a subject to discover facts or to reveal new information
making models	creating representations of complex objects or processes
observing	using one or more of your senses to gather information
predicting	making a statement or claim about what will happen based on past experience or evidence

Scientific Attitudes

Curiosity often drives scientists to learn about the world around them. Creativity is useful for coming up with inventive ways to solve problems. Such qualities and attitudes, and the ability to keep an open mind, are essential for scientists.

When sharing results or findings, honesty and ethics are also essential. Ethics refers to rules for knowing right from wrong.

Being skeptical is also important. This means having doubts about things based on past experiences and evidence. Skepticism helps to prevent accepting data and results that may not be true.

Scientists must also avoid bias—likes or dislikes of people, ideas, or things. They must avoid experimental bias, which is a mistake that may make an experiment's preferred outcome more likely.

Scientific Reasoning

Scientific reasoning depends on being logical and objective. When you are objective, you use evidence and apply logic to draw conclusions. Being subjective means basing conclusions on personal feelings, biases, or opinions. Subjective reasoning can interfere with science and skew results. Objective reasoning helps scientists use observations to reach conclusions about the natural world.

Scientists use two types of objective reasoning: deductive and inductive. Deductive reasoning involves starting with a general idea or theory and applying it to a situation. For example, the theory of plate tectonics indicates that earthquakes happen mostly where tectonic plates meet. You could then draw the conclusion, or deduce, that California has many earthquakes because tectonic plates meet there.

In inductive reasoning, you make a generalization from a specific observation. When scientists collect data in an experiment and draw a conclusion based on that data, they use inductive reasoning. For example, if fertilizer causes one set of plants to grow faster than another, you might infer that the fertilizer promotes plant growth.

Make Meaning
Think about a bias the marine biologist in the photo could show that results in paying more or less attention to one kind of organism over others. Make a prediction about how that bias could affect the biologist's survey of the coral reef.

Write About It
Suppose it is raining when you go to sleep one night. When you wake up the next morning, you observe frozen puddles on the ground and icicles on tree branches. Use scientific reasoning to draw a conclusion about the air temperature outside. Support your conclusion using deductive or inductive reasoning.

SEP.1, SEP.2, SEP.3, SEP.4, CCC.4

Science Processes

Scientific Inquiry

Scientists contribute to scientific knowledge by conducting investigations and drawing conclusions. The process often begins with an observation that leads to a question, which is then followed by the development of a hypothesis. This is known as scientific inquiry.

One of the first steps in scientific inquiry is asking questions. However, it's important to make a question specific with a narrow focus so the investigation will not be too broad. A biologist may want to know all there is to know about wolves, for example. But a good, focused question for a specific inquiry might be "How many offspring does the average female wolf produce in her lifetime?"

A hypothesis is a possible answer to a scientific question. A hypothesis must be testable. For something to be testable, researchers must be able to carry out an investigation and gather evidence that will either support or disprove the hypothesis.

Scientific Models

Models are tools that scientists use to study phenomena indirectly. A model is any representation of an object or process. Illustrations, dioramas, globes, diagrams, computer programs, and mathematical equations are all examples of scientific models. For example, a diagram of Earth's crust and mantle can help you to picture layers deep below the surface and understand events such as volcanic eruptions.

Models also allow scientists to represent objects that are either very large, such as our solar system, or very small, such as a molecule of DNA. Models can also represent processes that occur over a long period of time, such as the changes that have occurred throughout Earth's history.

Reflect Identify the benefits and limitations of using a plastic model of DNA, as shown here.

Models are helpful, but they have limitations. Physical models are not made of the same materials as the objects they represent. Most models of complex objects or processes show only major parts, stages, or relationships. Many details are left out. Therefore, you may not be able to learn as much from models as you would through direct observation.

Science Experiments

An experiment or investigation must be well planned to produce valid results. In planning an experiment, you must identify the independent and dependent variables. You must also do as much as possible to remove the effects of other variables. A controlled experiment is one in which you test only one variable at a time.

For example, suppose you plan a controlled experiment to learn how the type of material affects the speed at which sound waves travel through it. The only variable that should change is the type of material. This way, if the speed of sound changes, you know that it is a result of a change in the material, not another variable such as the thickness of the material or the type of sound used.

You should also remove bias from any investigation. You may inadvertently introduce bias by selecting subjects you like and avoiding those you don't like. Scientists often conduct investigations by taking random samples to avoid ending up with biased results.

Once you plan your investigation and begin to collect data, it's important to record and organize the data. You may wish to use a graph to display and help you to interpret the data.

Communicating is the sharing of ideas and results with others through writing and speaking. Communicating data and conclusions is a central part of science.

Scientists share knowledge, including new findings, theories, and techniques for collecting data. Conferences, journals, and websites help scientists to communicate with each other. Popular media, including newspapers, magazines, and social media sites, help scientists to share their knowledge with nonscientists. However, before the results of investigations are shared and published, other scientists should review the experiment for possible sources of error, such as bias and unsupported conclusions.

Write About It
List four ways you could communicate the results of a scientific study about the health of sea turtles in the Pacific Ocean.

SEP.1, SEP.6, SEP.7, SEP.8

Scientific Knowledge

Scientific Explanations

Suppose you learn that adult flamingos are pink because of the food they eat. This statement is a scientific explanation—it describes how something in nature works or explains why it happens. Scientists from different fields use methods such as researching information, designing experiments, and making models to form scientific explanations. Scientific explanations often result from many years of work and multiple investigations conducted by many scientists.

Scientific Theories and Laws

A scientific law is a statement that describes what you can expect to occur every time under a particular set of conditions. A scientific law describes an observed pattern in nature, but it does not attempt to explain it. For example, the law of superposition describes what you can expect to find in terms of the ages of layers of rock. Geologists use this observed pattern to determine the relative ages of sedimentary rock layers. But the law does not explain why the pattern occurs.

By contrast, a scientific theory is a well-tested explanation for a wide range of observations or experimental results. It provides details and describes causes of observed patterns. Something is elevated to a theory only when there is a large body of evidence that supports it. However, a scientific theory can be changed or overturned when new evidence is found.

✍ Write About It
Choose two fields of science that interest you. Describe a method used to develop scientific explanations in each field.

SEP Construct Explanations Complete the table to compare and contrast a scientific theory and a scientific law.

	Scientific Theory	Scientific Law
Definition		
Does it attempt to explain a pattern observed in nature?		

Analyzing Scientific Explanations

To analyze scientific explanations that you hear on the news or read in a book such as this one, you need scientific literacy. Scientific literacy means understanding scientific terms and principles well enough to ask questions, evaluate information, and make decisions. Scientific reasoning gives you a process to apply. This includes looking for bias and errors in the research, evaluating data, and identifying faulty reasoning. For example, by evaluating how a survey was conducted, you may find a serious flaw in the researchers' methods.

Evidence and Opinions

The basis for scientific explanations is empirical evidence. Empirical evidence includes the data and observations that have been collected through scientific processes. Satellite images, photos, and maps of mountains and volcanoes are all examples of empirical evidence that support a scientific explanation about Earth's tectonic plates. Scientists look for patterns when they analyze this evidence. For example, they might see a pattern that mountains and volcanoes often occur near tectonic plate boundaries.

To evaluate scientific information, you must first distinguish between evidence and opinion. In science, evidence includes objective observations and conclusions that have been repeated. Evidence may or may not support a scientific claim. An opinion is a subjective idea that is formed from evidence, but it cannot be confirmed by evidence.

Write About It
Suppose the conservation committee of a town wants to gauge residents' opinions about a proposal to stock the local ponds with fish every spring. The committee pays for a survey to appear on a web site that is popular with people who like to fish. The results of the survey show 78 people in favor of the proposal and two against it. Do you think the survey's results are valid? Explain.

Make Meaning
Explain what empirical evidence the photograph reveals.

SEP.3, SEP.4

Tools of Science

Measurement

Making measurements using standard units is important in all fields of science. This allows scientists to repeat and reproduce other experiments, as well as to understand the precise meaning of the results of others. Scientists use a measurement system called the International System of Units, or SI.

For each type of measurement, there is a series of units that are greater or less than each other. The unit a scientist uses depends on what is being measured. For example, a geophysicist tracking the movements of tectonic plates may use centimeters, as plates tend to move small amounts each year. Meanwhile, a marine biologist might measure the movement of migrating bluefin tuna on the scale of kilometers.

Units for length, mass, volume, and density are based on powers of ten—a meter is equal to 100 centimeters or 1000 millimeters. Units of time do not follow that pattern. There are 60 seconds in a minute, 60 minutes in an hour, and 24 hours in a day. These units are based on patterns that humans perceived in nature. Units of temperature are based on scales that are set according to observations of nature. For example, 0°C is the temperature at which pure water freezes, and 100°C is the temperature at which it boils.

Write About It

Suppose you are planning an investigation in which you must measure the dimensions of several small mineral samples that fit in your hand. Which metric unit or units will you most likely use? Explain your answer.

Measurement	Metric units
Length or distance	meter (m), kilometer (km), centimeter (cm), millimeter (mm) 1 km = 1,000 m 1 cm = 10 mm 1 m = 100 cm
Mass	kilogram (kg), gram (g), milligram (mg) 1 kg = 1,000 g 1 g = 1,000 mg
Volume	cubic meter (m³), cubic centimeter (cm³) 1 m³ = 1,000,000 cm³
Density	kilogram per cubic meter (kg/m³), gram per cubic centimeter (g/cm³) 1,000 kg/m³ = 1 g/cm³
Temperature	degrees Celsius (°C), kelvin (K) 1°C = 273 K
Time	hour (h), minute (m), second (s)

Math Skills

Using numbers to collect and interpret data involves math skills that are essential in science. For example, you use math skills when you estimate the number of birds in an entire forest after counting the actual number of birds in ten trees.

Scientists evaluate measurements and estimates for their precision and accuracy. In science, an accurate measurement is very close to the actual value. Precise measurements are very close, or nearly equal, to each other. Reliable measurements are both accurate and precise. An imprecise value may be a sign of an error in data collection. This kind of anomalous data may be excluded to avoid skewing the data and harming the investigation.

Other math skills include performing specific calculations, such as finding the mean, or average, value in a data set. The mean can be calculated by adding up all of the values in the data set and then dividing that sum by the number of values.

Hour	Number of Ducks Observed at a Pond
1	12
2	10
3	2
4	14
5	13
6	10
7	11

SEP Use Mathematics The data table shows how many ducks were seen at a pond every hour over the course of seven hours. Is there a data point that seems anomalous? If so, cross out that data point. Then, calculate the mean number of ducks on the pond. Round the mean to the nearest whole number.

Graphs

Graphs help scientists to interpret data by helping them to find trends or patterns in the data. A line graph displays data that show how one variable (the dependent or outcome variable) changes in response to another (the independent or test variable). The slope and shape of a graph line can reveal patterns and help scientists to make predictions. For example, line graphs can help you to spot patterns of change over time.

Scientists use bar graphs to compare data across categories or subjects that may not affect each other. The heights of the bars make it easy to compare those quantities. A circle graph, also known as a pie chart, shows the proportions of different parts of a whole.

Write About It
You and a friend record the distance you travel every 15 minutes on a one-hour bike trip. Your friend wants to display the data as a circle graph. Explain whether or not this is the best type of graph to display your data. If not, suggest another graph to use.

SEP.1, SEP.2, SEP.3, SEP.6

The Engineering Design Process

Engineers are builders and problem solvers. Chemical engineers experiment with new fuels made from algae. Civil engineers design roadways and bridges. Bioengineers develop medical devices and prosthetics. The common trait among engineers is an ability to identify problems and design solutions to solve them. Engineers use a creative process that relies on scientific methods to help guide them from a concept or idea all the way to the final product.

Define the Problem

To identify or define a problem, different questions need to be asked: *What are the effects of the problem? What are the likely causes? What other factors could be involved?* Sometimes the obvious, immediate cause of a problem may be the result of another problem that may not be immediately apparent. For example, climate change results in different weather patterns, which in turn can affect organisms that live in certain habitats. So engineers must be aware of all the possible effects of potential solutions. Engineers must also take into account how well different solutions deal with the different causes of the problem.

Reflect Write about a problem that you encountered in your life that had both immediate, obvious causes as well as less-obvious and less-immediate ones.

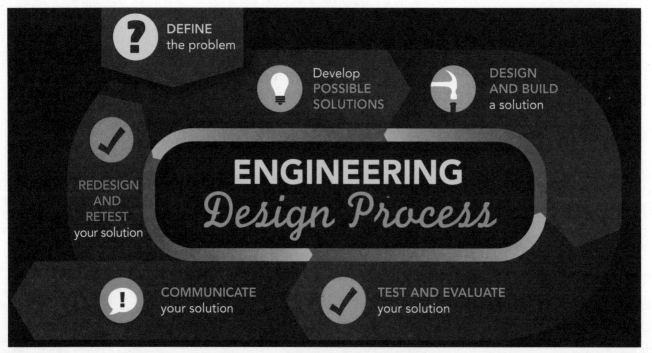

DEFINE the problem

Develop POSSIBLE SOLUTIONS

DESIGN AND BUILD a solution

REDESIGN AND RETEST your solution

ENGINEERING *Design Process*

COMMUNICATE your solution

TEST AND EVALUATE your solution

As engineers consider problems and design solutions, they must identify and categorize the criteria and constraints of the project.

Criteria are the factors that must be met or accomplished by the solution. For example, a gardener who wants to protect outdoor plants from deer and rabbits may say that the criteria for the solution are "plants are no longer eaten" and "plant growth is not inhibited in any way." The gardener then knows the plants cannot simply be sealed off from the environment, because the plants will not receive sunlight and water.

The same gardener will likely have constraints on his solution, such as budget for materials and time that is available for working on the project. By setting constraints, a solution can be designed that will be successful without introducing a new set of problems. No one wants to spend $500 on materials to protect $100 worth of tomatoes and cucumbers.

Develop Possible Solutions

After the problem has been identified, and the criteria and constraints identified, an engineer will consider possible solutions. This often involves working in teams with other engineers and designers to brainstorm ideas and research materials that can be used in the design.

It's important for engineers to think creatively and explore all potential solutions. If you wanted to design a bicycle that was safer and easier to ride than a traditional bicycle, then you would want more than just one or two solutions. Having multiple ideas to choose from increases the likelihood that you will develop a solution that meets the criteria and constraints. In addition, different ideas that result from brainstorming can often lead to new and better solutions to an existing problem.

Make Meaning
Using the example of a garden that is vulnerable to wild animals such as deer, make a list of likely constraints on an engineering solution to the problem you identified before. Determine if there are common traits among the constraints, and identify categories for them.

Design a Solution

Engineers then develop the idea that they feel best solves the problem. Once a solution has been chosen, engineers and designers get to work building a model or prototype of the solution. A model may involve sketching on paper or using computer software to construct a model of the solution. A prototype is a working model of the solution.

Building a model or prototype helps an engineer determine whether a solution meets the criteria and stays within the constraints. During this stage of the process, engineers must often deal with new problems and make any necessary adjustments to the model or prototype.

Test and Evaluate a Solution

Whether testing a model or a prototype, engineers use scientific processes to evaluate their solutions. Multiple experiments, tests, or trials are conducted, data are evaluated, and results and analyses are communicated. New criteria or constraints may emerge as a result of testing. In most cases, a solution will require some refinement or revision, even if it has been through successful testing. Refining a solution is necessary if there are new constraints, such as less money or available materials. Additional testing may be done to ensure that a solution satisfies local, state, or federal laws or standards.

Make Meaning Think about an aluminum beverage can. What would happen if the price or availability of aluminum changed so much that cans needed to be made of a new material? What would the criteria and constraints be on the development of a new can?

A naval architect sets up a model to test how the the hull's design responds to waves.

Communicate the Solution

Engineers need to communicate the final design to the people who will manufacture the product. This may include sketches, detailed drawings, computer simulations, and written text. Engineers often provide evidence that was collected during the testing stage. This evidence may include graphs and data tables that support the decisions made for the final design.

If there is feedback about the solution, then the engineers and designers must further refine the solution. This might involve making minor adjustments to the design, or it might mean bigger modifications to the design based on new criteria or constraints. Any changes in the design will require additional testing to make sure that the changes work as intended.

Redesign and Retest the Solution

At different steps in the engineering and design process, a solution usually must be revised and retested. Many designs fail to work perfectly, even after models and prototypes are built, tested, and evaluated. Engineers must be ready to analyze new results and deal with any new problems that arise. Troubleshooting, or fixing design problems, allows engineers to adjust the design to improve on how well the solution meets the need.

SEP Communicate Information Suppose you are an engineer at an aerospace company. Your team is designing a rover to be used on a future NASA space mission. A family member doesn't understand why so much of your team's time is taken up with testing and retesting the rover design. What are three things you would tell your relative to explain why testing and retesting are so important to the engineering and design process?

....

....

....

....

....

....

....

....

....

Safety Symbols

These symbols warn of possible dangers in the laboratory and remind you to work carefully.

 Safety Goggles Wear safety goggles to protect your eyes in any activity involving chemicals, flames or heating, or glassware.

 Lab Apron Wear a laboratory apron to protect your skin and clothing from damage.

 Breakage Handle breakable materials, such as glassware, with care. Do not touch broken glassware.

 Heat-Resistant Gloves Use an oven mitt or other hand protection when handling hot materials, such as hot plates or hot glassware.

 Plastic Gloves Wear disposable plastic gloves when working with harmful chemicals and organisms. Keep your hands away from your face, and dispose of the gloves according to your teacher's instructions.

 Heating Use a clamp or tongs to pick up hot glassware. Do not touch hot objects with your bare hands.

 Flames Before you work with flames, tie back loose hair and clothing. Follow your teacher's instructions about lighting and extinguishing flames.

 No Flames When using flammable materials, make sure there are no flames, sparks, or other exposed heat sources present.

 Corrosive Chemical Avoid getting acid or other corrosive chemicals on your skin or clothing or in your eyes. Do not inhale the vapors. Wash your hands after the activity.

 Poison Do not let any poisonous chemical come into contact with your skin, and do not inhale its vapors. Wash your hands when you are finished with the activity.

 Fumes Work in a well-ventilated area when harmful vapors may be involved. Avoid inhaling vapors directly. Test an odor only when directed to do so by your teacher, and use a wafting motion to direct the vapor toward your nose.

 Sharp Object Scissors, scalpels, knives, needles, pins, and tacks can cut your skin. Always direct a sharp edge or point away from yourself and others.

 Animal Safety Treat live or preserved animals or animal parts with care to avoid harming the animals or yourself. Wash your hands when you are finished with the activity.

 Plant Safety Handle plants only as directed by your teacher. If you are allergic to certain plants, tell your teacher; do not do an activity involving those plants. Avoid touching harmful plants such as poison ivy. Wash your hands when you are finished with the activity.

 Electric Shock To avoid electric shock, never use electrical equipment around water, when the equipment is wet, or when your hands are wet. Be sure cords are untangled and cannot trip anyone. Unplug equipment not in use.

 Physical Safety When an experiment involves physical activity, avoid injuring yourself or others. Alert your teacher if there is any reason you should not participate.

 Disposal Dispose of chemicals and other laboratory materials safely. Follow the instructions from your teacher.

 Hand Washing Wash your hands thoroughly when finished with an activity. Use soap and warm water. Rinse well.

 General Safety Awareness When this symbol appears, follow the instructions provided. When you are asked to develop your own procedure in a lab, have your teacher approve your plan.

Using a Laboratory Balance

The laboratory balance is an important tool in scientific investigations. Different kinds of balances are used in the laboratory to determine the masses and weights of objects. You can use a triple-beam balance to determine the masses of materials that you study or experiment with in the laboratory. An electronic balance, unlike a triple-beam balance, is used to measure the weights of materials.

The triple-beam balance that you may use in your science class is probably similar to the balance depicted in this Appendix. To use the balance properly, you should learn the name, location, and function of each part of the balance.

Triple-Beam Balance

The triple-beam balance is a single-pan balance with three beams calibrated in grams. The back, or 100-gram, beam is divided into ten units of 10 grams each. The middle, or 500-gram, beam is divided into five units of 100 grams each. The front, or 10-gram, beam is divided into ten units of 1 gram each. Each gram on the front beam is further divided into units of 0.1 gram.

Apply Concepts What is the greatest mass you could find with the triple-beam balance in the picture?

....

Calculate What is the mass of the apple in the picture?

....

The following procedure can be used to find the mass of an object with a triple-beam balance:

1. Place the object on the pan.

2. Move the rider on the middle beam notch by notch until the horizontal pointer on the right drops below zero. Move the rider back one notch.

3. Move the rider on the back beam notch by notch until the pointer again drops below zero. Move the rider back one notch.

4. Slowly slide the rider along the front beam until the pointer stops at the zero point.

5. The mass of the object is equal to the sum of the readings on the three beams.

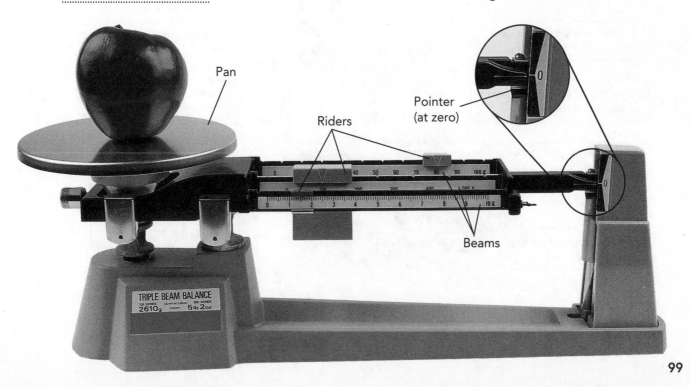

Pan

Riders

Pointer (at zero)

Beams

TRIPLE BEAM BALANCE
2610g   5 lb 2 oz

APPENDIX C

Using a Microscope

The microscope is an essential tool in the study of life science. It allows you to see things that are too small to be seen with the unaided eye.

You will probably use a compound microscope like the one you see here. The compound microscope has more than one lens that magnifies the object you view.

Typically, a compound microscope has one lens in the eyepiece (the part you look through). The eyepiece lens usually magnifies 10×. Any object you view through this lens will appear 10 times larger than it is.

A compound microscope may contain two or three other lenses called objective lenses. They are called the low-power and high-power objective lenses. The low-power objective lens usually magnifies 10×. The high-power objective lenses usually magnify 40× and 100×.

To calculate the total magnification with which you are viewing an object, multiply the magnification of the eyepiece lens by the magnification of the objective lens you are using. For example, the eyepiece's magnification of 10× multiplied by the low-power objective's magnification of 10× equals a total magnification of 100×.

Use the photo of the compound microscope to become familiar with the parts of the microscope and their functions.

The Parts of a Microscope

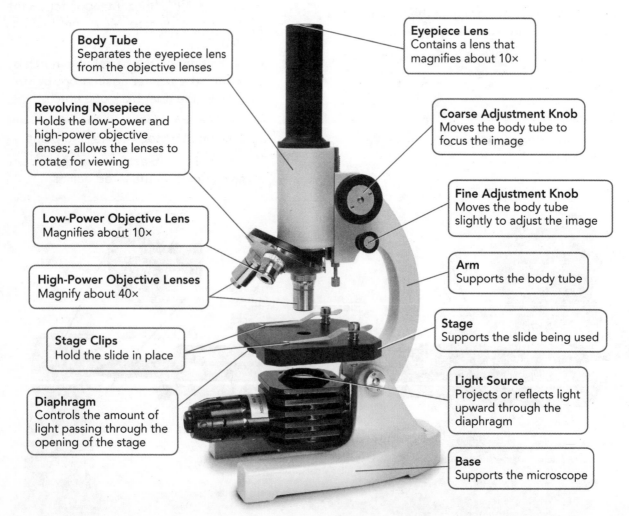

Body Tube
Separates the eyepiece lens from the objective lenses

Revolving Nosepiece
Holds the low-power and high-power objective lenses; allows the lenses to rotate for viewing

Low-Power Objective Lens
Magnifies about 10×

High-Power Objective Lenses
Magnify about 40×

Stage Clips
Hold the slide in place

Diaphragm
Controls the amount of light passing through the opening of the stage

Eyepiece Lens
Contains a lens that magnifies about 10×

Coarse Adjustment Knob
Moves the body tube to focus the image

Fine Adjustment Knob
Moves the body tube slightly to adjust the image

Arm
Supports the body tube

Stage
Supports the slide being used

Light Source
Projects or reflects light upward through the diaphragm

Base
Supports the microscope

Using the Microscope

Use the following procedures when you are working with a microscope.

1. To carry the microscope, grasp the microscope's arm with one hand. Place your other hand under the base.

2. Place the microscope on a table with the arm toward you.

3. Turn the coarse adjustment knob to raise the body tube.

4. Revolve the nosepiece until the low-power objective lens clicks into place.

5. Adjust the diaphragm. While looking through the eyepiece, adjust the mirror until you see a bright white circle of light. **CAUTION:** Never use direct sunlight as a light source.

6. Place a slide on the stage. Center the specimen over the opening on the stage. Use the stage clips to hold the slide in place. **CAUTION:** Glass slides are fragile.

7. Look at the stage from the side. Carefully turn the coarse adjustment knob to lower the body tube until the low-power objective almost touches the slide.

8. Looking through the eyepiece, very slowly turn the coarse adjustment knob until the specimen comes into focus.

9. To switch to the high-power objective lens, look at the microscope from the side. Carefully revolve the nosepiece until the high-power objective lens clicks into place. Make sure the lens does not hit the slide.

10. Looking through the eyepiece, turn the fine adjustment knob until the specimen comes into focus.

Making a Wet-Mount Slide

Use the following procedures to make a wet-mount slide of a specimen.

1. Obtain a clean microscope slide and a coverslip. **CAUTION:** Glass slides and coverslips are fragile.

2. Place the specimen on the center of the slide. The specimen must be thin enough for light to pass through it.

3. Using a plastic dropper, place a drop of water on the specimen.

4. Gently place one edge of the coverslip against the slide so that it touches the edge of the water drop at a 45° angle. Slowly lower the coverslip over the specimen. If you see air bubbles trapped beneath the coverslip, tap the coverslip gently with the eraser end of a pencil.

5. Remove any excess water at the edge of the coverslip with a paper towel.

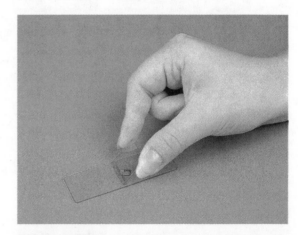

Periodic Table of Elements

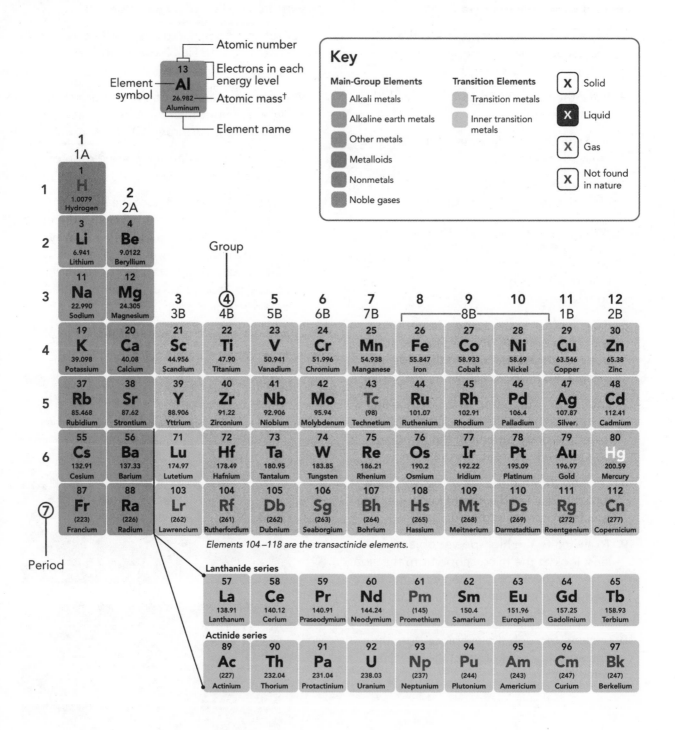

Elements 104–118 are the transactinide elements.

†*The atomic masses in parentheses are the mass numbers of the longest-lived isotope of elements for which a standard atomic mass cannot be defined.*

18 8A

13 3A	14 4A	15 5A	16 6A	17 7A	2 He 4.0026 Helium
5 B 10.81 Boron	6 C 12.011 Carbon	7 N 14.007 Nitrogen	8 O 15.999 Oxygen	9 F 18.998 Fluorine	10 Ne 20.179 Neon
13 Al 26.982 Aluminum	14 Si 28.086 Silicon	15 P 30.974 Phosphorus	16 S 32.06 Sulfur	17 Cl 35.453 Chlorine	18 Ar 39.948 Argon
31 Ga 69.72 Gallium	32 Ge 72.59 Germanium	33 As 74.922 Arsenic	34 Se 78.96 Selenium	35 Br 79.904 Bromine	36 Kr 83.80 Krypton
49 In 114.82 Indium	50 Sn 118.69 Tin	51 Sb 121.75 Antimony	52 Te 127.60 Tellurium	53 I 126.90 Iodine	54 Xe 131.30 Xenon
81 Tl 204.37 Thallium	82 Pb 207.2 Lead	83 Bi 208.98 Bismuth	84 Po (209) Polonium	85 At (210) Astatine	86 Rn (222) Radon
113 Nh (284) Nihonium	114 Fl (289) Flerovium	115 Mc (288) Moscovium	116 Lv (292) Livermorium	117 Ts (294) Tennessine	118 Og (294) Oganesson

66 Dy 162.50 Dysprosium	67 Ho 164.93 Holmium	68 Er 167.26 Erbium	69 Tm 168.93 Thulium	70 Yb 173.04 Ytterbium
98 Cf (251) Californium	99 Es (252) Einsteinium	100 Fm (257) Fermium	101 Md (258) Mendelevium	102 No (259) Nobelium

GLOSSARY

A

atom The basic particle from which all elements are made; the smallest particle of an element that has the properties of that element. (8)

B

boiling point The temperature at which a liquid boils. (60)

Boyle's Law A principle that describes the relationship between the pressure and volume of a gas at constant temperature. (71)

C

Charles's Law A principle that describes the relationship between the temperature and volume of a gas at constant pressure. (69)

chemical change A change in which one or more substances combine or break apart to form new substances. (27)

chemical property A characteristic of a substance that describes its ability to change into different substances. (7)

compound A substance made of two or more elements chemically combined in a specific ratio, or proportion. (10)

condensation The change in state from a gas to a liquid. (62)

D

density The measurement of how much mass of a substance is contained in a given volume. (18)

E

element A pure substance that cannot be broken down into other substances by chemical or physical means. (8)

evaporation The process by which molecules at the surface of a liquid absorb enough energy to change to a gas. (60)

F

freezing point The temperature at which a liquid freezes. (59)

G

gas A state of matter with no definite shape or volume. (53)

L

liquid A state of matter that has no definite shape but has a definite volume. (51)

M

mass A measure of how much matter is in an object. (15)

matter Anything that has mass and takes up space. (5)

melting point The temperature at which a substance changes from a solid to a liquid; the same as the freezing point, or temperature at which a liquid changes to a solid. (58)

mixture Two or more substances that are together in the same place but their atoms are not chemically bonded. (11)

molecule A neutral group of two or more atoms held together by covalent bonds. (9)

P

physical change A change that alters the form or appearance of a material but does not make the material into another substance. (25)

physical property A characteristic of a pure substance that can be observed without changing it into another substance. (6)

pressure The force pushing on a surface divided by the area of that surface. (67)

S

solid A state of matter that has a definite shape and a definite volume. (48)

sublimation The change in state from a solid directly to a gas without passing through the liquid state. (63)

substance A single kind of matter that is pure and has a specific set of properties. (5)

surface tension The result of an inward pull among the molecules of a liquid that brings the molecules on the surface closer together; causes the surface to act as if it has a thin skin. (52)

T

temperature How hot or cold something is; a measure of the average energy of motion of the particles of a substance; the measure of the average kinetic energy of the particles of a substance. (57)

thermal energy The total kinetic and potential energy of all the particles of an object. (57)

V

vaporization The change of state from a liquid to a gas. (60)

viscosity A liquid's resistance to flowing. (52)

volume The amount of space that matter occupies. (15)

W

weight A measure of the force of gravity acting on an object. (15)

INDEX

Page numbers for key terms are printed in boldface type.

CREDITS

Photographs

Photo locators denoted as follows: Top (T), Center (C), Bottom (B), Left (L), Right (R), Background (Bkgd)

Covers

Front Cover: Frank Krahmer/Getty Images
Back Cover: LHF Graphics/Shutterstock

Front Matter

iv: Clari Massimiliano/Shutterstock; vi: Sokkajar/Fotolia; vii: Makieni/Fotolia; viii: Brian J. Skerry/National Geographic/Getty Images; ix: Gary Meszaros/Science Source/Getty Images;

Topic 1

x: Sokkajar/Fotolia;002: Stock_Colors/E+/Getty Images; 004: Sami Sarkis RM CC/Alamy Stock Photo; 006 Bkgrd: Lazyllama/Shutterstock; 006 BL: Subinpumsom/Fotolia; 007 BL: Borroko72/Fotolia; 007 BR: Arpad Nagy-Bagoly/Fotolia; 008 BR: Anyka/123RF; 008 C: James Steidl/Shutterstock; 010 TC: Smereka/Shutterstock; 010 TR: GIPhotoStock/Science Source; 011 TCR: Bert Folsom/123RF; 011 TR: Lepas2004/iStock/Getty Images; 013 BC: SuperStock; 013 Bkgrd: Massimo Pizzotti/ AGE Fotostock/Superstock; 013 TR: David L. Ryan/The Boston Globe/Getty Images; 014: Michelle McMahon/Moment/Getty Images; 016 T: Martin Shields/Alamy Stock Photo; 016 TR: Martin Shields/Alamy Stock Photo; 017 BR: Leungchopan/ Fotolia; 017 CR: GIPhotoStock/Science Source; 017 L: Hitandrun IKON Images/Newscom; 018: SchulteProductions/ E+/Getty Images; 020 CR: RF Company/Alamy Stock Photo; 020 L: Denis Radovanovic/Shutterstock; 020 R: Siim Sepp/ Alamy Stock Photo; 020 T: Victor21041958/Fotolia; 022: U.S. Coast Guard; 025: Fuse/Corbis/Getty Images; 026: Sergey Dobrydnev/Shutterstock; 027 BCL: Vinicef/Alamy Stock Photo; 027 BCR: Vinicef/Alamy Stock Photo; 027 BL: Stephanie Frey/ Fotolia; 027 BR: Kzen/Shutterstock; 027 BR: Shaiith/iStock/ Getty Images; 028 CL: Fuse/Corbis/Getty Images; 028 CR: Charles D. Winters/Science Source; 028 TL: Studio on line/ Shutterstock; 028 TR: 123RF; 030 Bkgrd: Peter Barritt/Alamy Stock Photo; 030 BL: Paul Souders/Alamy Stock Photo; 031: Byrdyak/123RF; 033: Kiyoshi Takahase Segundo/Alamy Stock Photo; 038: Torontonian/Alamy Stock Photo; 039: USantos/ Fotolia;

Topic 2

042: Makieni/Fotolia; 044: Studio 8/Pearson Education Ltd.; 046: Kendall Rittenour/Shutterstock; 048: Dmytro Skorobogatov/Alamy Stock Photo; 049 BL: Marco Cavina/ Shutterstock; 049 BR: CrackerClips Stock Media/Shutterstock; 049 T: Erika8213/Fotolia; 050 BCL: Robyn Mackenzie/ Shutterstock; 050 BL: Fototrips/Fotolia; 051 BL: Kropic/Fotolia; 051 BR: Rony Zmiri/Fotolia; 052 BL: Wiklander/Shutterstock; 052 BR: Oriori/Fotolia; 053 T: Sutichak/Fotolia; 053 TL: Hudiemm/Getty Images; 055 BCR: Özgür Güvenç/Fotolia; 055 CR: Xiaoliangge/Fotolia; 056: WavebreakMediaMicro/ Fotolia; 060 TC: PhotoAlto/Odilon Dimier/Getty Images; 060 TL: Petr Malyshev/Fotolia; 060 TR: Uygaar/Getty Images; 062 B: Michael Hare/Shutterstock; 062 CR: Cultura Creative (RF)/ Alamy Stock Photo; 063: Charles D. Winters/Science Source; 066: Ronstik/Fotolia; 068 T: Saap585/Shutterstock; 068 TC: Eric Audras/PhotoAlto/Age Fotostock; 068 TL: Gudellaphoto/ Fotolia; 068 TR: Peterspiro/iStock/Getty Images; 071: Cebas/ Shutterstock; 073 B: Faded Beauty/Fotolia; 073 CL: Alex-mit/ iStock/Getty Images; 076 Bkgrd: Physicx/Shutterstock; 076 BL: Mara Zemgaliete/Fotolia; 076 TL: Denisfilm/Fotolia; 078 BC: Pakhnyushcha/Shutterstock; 078 C: Reika/Shutterstock; 078 CR: Richard Megna/Fundamental Photographs; 082: Mrallen/ Fotolia; 083: Bestphotostudio/Fotolia;

End Matter

086 TCL: Cyndi Monaghan/Getty Images; BL: EHStockphoto/ Shutterstock; TL: Javier Larrea/AGE Fotostock; BCL: Philippe Plailly & Elisabeth Daynes/Science Source; 087: WaterFrame/ Alamy Stock Photo; 088: Africa Studio/Shutterstock; 089: Jeff Rotman/Alamy Stock Photo; 090: Grant Faint/Getty Images; 091: Ross Armstrong/Alamy Stock Photo; 092: Geoz/Alamy Stock Photo; 095: Martin Shields/Alamy Stock Photo; 096: Nicola Tree/Getty Images; 097: Regan Geeseman/NASA; 099: Pearson Education Ltd.; 100: Pearson Education Ltd.; 101 BR: Pearson Education Ltd.; 101TR: Pearson Education Ltd.

Program graphics: ArtMari/Shutterstock; BeatWalk/ Shutterstock; Irmun/Shutterstock; LHF Graphics/Shutterstock; Multigon/Shutterstock; Nikolaeva/Shutterstock; silm/ Shutterstock; Undrey/Shutterstock

Use this space for recording notes and sketching out ideas.

Take Notes

Use this space for recording notes and sketching out ideas.

Use this space for recording notes and sketching out ideas.

Take Notes

Use this space for recording notes and sketching out ideas.